Reading Renaissance
POWER LESSONS

**Literature-Based Lessons
to Teach Reading Skills**

GRADE 4

ACKNOWLEDGMENTS
For planning and writing the lessons: Dottie Raymer and Jennifer Jacobson.
For creating the illustrations: Stephanie Parish.

For the K-W-L Interactive Reading Strategy: Donna Ogle, Ed. D. From "K-W-L: A Teaching Model That Develops Active Reading of Expository Text," *The Reading Teacher*, February 1986, pp. 564–570. Reprinted by permission of Donna Ogle, Ed. D., National-Louis University.

For "The Crocodile" by Michael Flanders: Henry Holt and Company, LLC, from CREATURES GREAT AND SMALL by Michael Flanders. Text copyright, © 1964, 1992 by Michael Flanders. Reprinted by permission of Henry Holt and Company, LLC.

Accelerated Reader and the Renaissance Learning logo are registered trademarks of Renaissance Learning, Inc. Reading Renaissance is a registered trademark of the School Renaissance Institute, Inc. AR, Duolog Reading, TOPS, Renaissance, and Power Lessons are trademarks of Renaissance Learning, Inc.

ISBN 1-893751-07-4
© 2000, Renaissance Learning, Inc.
All rights reserved.

This publication is protected by U.S. and international copyright laws. It is unlawful to duplicate or reproduce any copyrighted material without authorization from the copyright holder. Certain forms that may be reproduced for use by teachers within their own school are marked "Reproducible Form." They are not to be reproduced for private consulting or commercial use. For more information, contact:

Renaissance Learning
P.O. Box 45016
Madison, WI 53744-5016
(800) 200-4848

Contents

Introduction
Power Lessons and Reading Renaissance 1
What Are Power Lessons? 1
Power Lessons and the Reading Renaissance Workshop 2
Creating Power Lessons 2
Where Do Ideas for Power Lessons Come From? 5
Power Lessons: Grade 4 5

Reading Renaissance Skills
Using ZPD 7
Using the TOPS Report 10
Using the Student Reading Log 12
Setting Goals 15

Comprehension Strategies
Author's Purpose 18
Classifying and Categorizing 20
Compare and Contrast 22
Drawing Conclusions 24
Fact and Opinion 26
Main Idea and Details 28
Making Generalizations 30
Multiple Causes and Effects 32
Predicting Outcomes 34
Previewing and Setting a Purpose 36
Self-Correction Strategies 38
Sequence 40
Summarizing Nonfiction 42
Text Features: Headings and Subheadings 44

Author's Craft
Imagery 46
Similes and Metaphors 48

Story Elements
Characterization 50
Plot: Conflict and Resolution 52
Setting 54
Theme 56
Tone 58

Genre
Biography and Autobiography 60
Historical Fiction 62

Vocabulary Strategies
Context Clues 64
Homonyms 66
Synonyms and Antonyms 68

Phonics and Word Study
Consonant Variants 70
Prefixes That Mean "Not" 72
Suffixes 74
Syllabication 76

Study Skills
Dictionary Skills 78
Library Skills 80
Note Taking 82
Parts of a Book 84
Selecting Reference Materials 86
Using Maps and Charts 88

Reproducible Forms
Power Lesson Planning Form 92
Syllabication Rules 93
Student Reading Log 94
Primary Student Reading Log 95
Goal-Setting Chart 96
Sample TOPS Report 97
Student Reading Plan 98

List of Books Referred to in the Lessons 99

Index of Skills Taught 100

Index of Accelerated Reader Literacy Skills Taught 103

Introduction

Power Lessons and Reading Renaissance

The goal of all reading instruction is to help students become lifelong learners who love to read. Research tells us that in order for this to happen, students must spend a substantial amount of time reading books. Using the power of learning information systems, Reading Renaissance enables you to manage this kind of extensive, literature-based reading practice. As a result, students' reading skills grow. At the same time, students are introduced to the wonderful world of books and develop a love of reading and learning that will serve them well throughout their lifetime.

For many schools, however, the notion of devoting so much time to literature-based reading practice is new, even anxiety provoking. The first question most teachers ask is, "How can I give my students the time for reading practice that they need every day and still teach the reading skills that I know are needed and that our curriculum requires me to teach?"

The answer is power lessons. Short and sharply focused, power lessons can be used to teach nearly every skill, and they accommodate various teaching styles and instructional techniques. Teachers who use power lessons find that these lessons are critical to teaching students the skills they need to learn and to giving students the time they need to transfer and practice those skills.

What Are Power Lessons?

Power lessons have three basic characteristics:
1. They are brief.
2. They deal with a single objective.
3. They are integrated with the books that students are reading on their own.

The format is straightforward. You present a skill, using examples from books with which students are familiar—often books that you are currently reading aloud to them. Students look for additional examples in their own books. During reading practice time, which usually follows the power lesson, you take Status of the Class. As you talk to each student individually, you check to see if they have understood the lesson and help them apply the skill to their own reading.

Power lessons are not, of course, a new concept. Many teachers have discovered that fifteen minutes is about as long as most students can focus on one idea or activity. Power lessons are, however, especially relevant to Reading Renaissance. As streamlined bursts of instruction, they free up time for the accountable reading practice that is the heart of Reading Renaissance. And as a literature-based instructional format, they keep the ultimate goal front and center: to help students perfect their skills so that they can more easily read for pleasure and learning.

Power Lessons and the Reading Renaissance Workshop

Power lessons are an important component of what we call the Reading Renaissance Workshop. This is the part of the school day that combines instruction, reading practice, and one-on-one contact with students. For a class of established readers, we suggest that you set aside 75 minutes a day, divided in the following manner:

Power Lesson. The short skill lesson you teach often will include reading to students and discussing a familiar book to give specific examples of the skill from literature.

Reading Practice Time. For established readers, we recommend sixty minutes of independent reading practice. During this time, students read silently, take Accelerated Reader Reading Practice quizzes, and select new books. If you choose to divide your sixty minutes into two or three periods daily, make sure that one of the periods immediately follows the power lesson.

Accelerated Reader Reading Practice Quizzes. After students complete books, they take quizzes. Quizzes motivate students to read and help you guide and monitor their reading progress.

Status of the Class. As students read independently, you visit individually with each student. Although this is a brief interaction, ranging from thirty seconds to perhaps a minute and a half, it provides you the opportunity to perform several key instructional tasks:

- Check to see that the student is able to apply the skill from the power lesson.
- Review the student reading log to monitor reading progress.
- Discuss the book that the student is currently reading.
- Intervene if the student is struggling with a concept or has chosen an inappropriate book.

Creating Power Lessons

The lessons included in this book are intended to be models as well as actual lessons that you can present to students. We encourage you to create your own power lessons. Page 4 summarizes the goals of each lesson step. You will notice that all power lessons have the following elements in common:

- **Power lessons are short.** A good power lesson takes only ten to fifteen minutes to present. When a skill is complex or has multiple parts, we suggest breaking the skill into sub-skills and presenting a series of lessons on that skill over the course of two or more days. You may also want to review a specific skill throughout the school year with periodic, brief power lessons.

- **Power lessons have a clear objective.** Since you have only fifteen minutes to present a skill, you must keep your objective firmly in mind. You will find that a power lesson works best when it has a single objective that is easily stated.

- **Power lessons rely on literature as the vehicle for instruction and practice.** When possible, use the book that you are currently reading aloud to students as a source of examples for the skill you are teaching. Ask students to look for examples in the books they are reading independently. Immediately follow the lesson with reading practice time, and direct students to look for additional examples as they read on their own. These assignments, however, should be simple and short so that students can stay focused on the meaning of the books they are reading. For example, while it would be a good idea to ask students to look for two examples of a compound word as they read, asking them to list all the compound words they can find would be distracting.

- **Skills taught in power lessons are assessed during Status of the Class.** As you talk to each student, ask questions that will help you determine whether the student has understood the lesson. After a lesson on cause and effect, for example, you might ask students, "What happened in the last chapter of your book? Why did it happen? What caused the character to feel this way? What was the effect of this character's actions?"

- **Skills taught in power lessons can be reinforced with other activities.** Each of the lessons in this book includes suggestions for added practice. You can use these practice activities during the days following the power lesson to reinforce the instruction, or you can use them later in the year as part of a power lesson that covers the same skill but uses a different book. You also might offer them to small groups of students who need more practice in a specific skill.

- **Power lessons are structured to get the most out of a short instruction period.** See "How to Create a Power Lesson" on page 4. You also may find it convenient to use the Power Lesson Planning Form on page 92.

How to Create a Power Lesson

Objective — State the lesson's objective in clear, concise terms. Generally, the simpler and more focused the objective is, the more successful the lesson will be.

Materials — If your current Read To book does not contain a good example of the skill or concept to be taught, choose another book that is familiar to all students. Another option is to choose a short book or story that can be read aloud in one sitting.

Lesson

1. Whenever possible, begin the lesson with a "hook" that relates the skill to be taught to students' lives. For example, you might use a listing that summarizes a popular television show to introduce the skill of summarizing.
2. Introduce the vocabulary or concept. Whenever possible, give an example from familiar, grade-appropriate literature.
3. Model the skill. Use graphic organizers, "think-alouds," and any other teaching strategies you have found to be successful with your students.
4. Give students a chance to try out the skill in a brief guided practice session. If you have used a graphic organizer in your lesson, have them help you complete the chart or diagram.
5. Sum up the lesson and direct students to apply the skill to their own reading or look for examples of the concept in books they are reading independently.

Status of the Class Follow-Up — List two or three questions that will help you determine whether the student has understood the lesson, such as:

- Can you find an example of ___ in your book?
- What words or details does the author use to support your conclusion?
- Did you run into any unfamiliar words? How did you figure them out?
- Does this book remind you of another book or something that happened in your own life?

Added Practice — Note activities you might use to give students additional practice in the skill, such as:

- Working together in cooperative-learning groups
- Using art, music, or movement to practice the skill
- Applying the skill to their own writing

Where Do Ideas for Power Lessons Come From?

You can use the power lesson format to teach word identification skills, vocabulary, comprehension, literary skills, and study skills, as well as Reading Renaissance routines and procedures. You will find ideas for creating power lessons in the same places you have found ideas for traditional lessons: basal readers, district or state curriculum guides, professional journals, and workshops. You will discover, too, that many of your favorite lessons can easily be transformed into power lessons by breaking them into smaller pieces and incorporating the power lesson elements listed earlier.

Power lessons can employ a variety of teaching strategies, including teacher modeling, K-W-L charts, story maps, and webs. Your choice of one over the other will depend on what you have found works best with your students. The important thing to remember about power lessons is that while the content and teaching strategy vary, the basic elements, as outlined, remain the same.

Power Lessons: Grade 4

The forty lessons in this book cover four basic Reading Renaissance routines and a selection of comprehension, literary, word identification, vocabulary, and study skills commonly taught at the fourth-grade level. If you are looking for a lesson on a specific skill not covered in this book, you may wish to adapt lessons from *Power Lessons: Grade 3* or *Power Lessons: Grade 5* or create a lesson of your own (see the Power Lesson Planning Form on page 92). Although we give examples from specific books that we believe are well suited to the lessons at each grade level, you can easily use other books with equal success, and we encourage you to do so. Most of all, we hope the lessons in this book will inspire you to present engaging, creative lessons that will help every one of your students discover the joy of reading.

Using ZPD

About Using ZPD

Practicing reading with books that are too hard results in frustration. Practicing reading with books that are too easy does little to improve skills and leads to boredom. We use a concept called the zone of proximal development (ZPD) to match students to appropriate books. A student's ZPD represents a level of difficulty that is neither too hard nor too easy, and is the level at which optimal learning takes place. For students who are reading on their own, you can identify ZPD in three ways:

1. If a student has used Accelerated Reader previously, start her out in the range of reading levels of books in which she scored between 85 and 92 percent on AR quizzes. You can find this information on her Student Record Report or on your class Diagnostic Report.
2. If a student is new to the program and you have a standardized reading test score available, refer to the Goal-Setting Chart on page 96. (The Goal-Setting Chart can also be printed out from the Accelerated Reader software, version 5.0 and higher.) Note that we give a ZPD range, as well as an average ZPD. This is because ZPD is a zone, not an exact number.
3. If a student has not used Accelerated Reader before, and you don't have a test score, estimate the student's reading level. Think about the level of basal reader the student is reading successfully or compare the student's reading ability to another student whose level you feel more sure of.

Carefully monitor Accelerated Reader Reading Practice quiz results. Once a student is consistently scoring between 85 and 92 percent (or higher) on books in his ZPD, consider moving him into higher-level books. If a student cannot maintain an average score of 85 to 92 percent on books in his ZPD, have the student try reading shorter books within that zone. If he is still not successful, move the student into lower-level books.

Remember, determining a student's zone of proximal development is not an exact science. Crucial to the success of Reading Renaissance is that you know each of your students—and that you use this knowledge thoughtfully to guide reading practice.

Students should be aware of their ZPD and know how to use it to select books. You will find this kind of involvement builds a sense of self-control in students and is highly motivating. You will also discover that students acquire an understanding of what is the right level of challenge for them. As a result, students themselves can provide valuable input as you set appropriate ZPDs.

Objective To help students use their ZPD reading levels to select books

Materials A variety of AR books about animals representing a wide range of reading levels (each book should be labeled with its reading level and AR point value); student reading log

Lesson

1. Ask, "You know you can catch a ball. Now, what kinds of throws might help you learn to catch a ball better?" As you discuss students' responses, be sure to include the following points:
   - Balls that are too easy to catch don't help you improve.
   - You might make an attempt at difficult balls—balls that are thrown too wide or high—but it probably won't be worth your effort.

2. Point out that practicing reading is like practicing any other skill. Display the AR books you've collected and ask, "Suppose you want to read a story about animals. How would you go about finding a book that is just right for you?" Possible responses include:
   - Look at the cover.
   - See how big the print is.
   - Read a little bit of it.

3. Tell students that sometimes it's difficult to know if a book is too easy or too hard just by looking at it. Then point to the reading label on one of the books and say, "These labels can help you make that decision." Explain that knowing how to use the reading level labels on AR books will help them choose books that are just right for them.

4. Write the letters ZPD on the board. Tell students that the letters stand for "zone of proximal development," a scientific name for an idea that can help students find the level at which they will get the most out of their reading practice. Remind students that just as people grow at different rates, their reading abilities grow at different rates. Stress that for this reason, each reader has her own individual ZPD level. Point out also that as each student's reading ability improves, the student will move into a new ZPD.

5. Show a sample student reading log (see page 94), and point out the space where the individual ZPD is written on the log. Point out that when students choose books, they should look at the label and compare the reading level to their ZPD.

6. Remind students that knowing their individual ZPD ranges and checking them against the book labels will help them choose books that are challenging but not too hard.

Status of the Class Follow-Up

As you take the Status of the Class, ask:
- What attracted you to this book?
- How did knowing your ZPD help you choose this book?
- Do you think we need to adjust your ZPD? Why?

Added Practice

- Students can make bookmarks on which they write their name and current ZPD. Suggest that students carry their bookmarks with them as they choose books to read.
- AR software can create customized book lists for each student based on her current ZPD level and other criteria. This may be a good time to give each student a customized list.

Using the TOPS Report

About the TOPS Report

Accelerated Reader reports give you meaningful information about your students' performance so that you can better match individuals to books, diagnose problems, provide appropriate intervention, and celebrate success. TOPS stands for "The Opportunity to Praise a Student." The report prints out immediately after a student finishes a Reading Practice quiz, giving the score for that quiz and points earned. The TOPS Report also indicates whether the book just quizzed on is fiction or nonfiction, and whether it was read to or with the student or whether the student read it independently. In addition, the TOPS Report notes the cumulative number of points earned, the number of quizzes taken and passed, and the student's average score. A sample TOPS Report can be found on page 97.

We strongly recommend that you instruct your students to show the TOPS Report to you immediately after they take a quiz. That way it will prompt a conversation, enabling you to give praise and guidance at the best possible moment.

We also encourage you to send TOPS Reports home with students. This will keep parents abreast of student progress and give them an opportunity to praise their child.

Objective

To help students use the TOPS Report to monitor their progress in reading

Materials

A copy of the TOPS Report for Jeremy Wallace for each student (page 97); Optional materials: An overhead projector and transparency of Jeremy Wallace's TOPS Report

Lesson

1. Write TOPS on the board, and ask students to speculate about what the initials stand for (The Opportunity to Praise a Student). Tell students that TOPS Reports print out immediately after they finish a Reading Practice quiz—therefore, every time they get a TOPS Report, they have the opportunity to be praised!

2. Direct students' attention to the TOPS Report for Jeremy Wallace. Tell them that this report is for an imaginary student who is in the fifth grade. Point out the sentences in dark type at the top of the page and have a volunteer read them aloud. Ask:
   - What does this statement tell us? Did Jeremy pass the quiz? (yes)
   - What book was the quiz on? (*Will You Sign Here, John Hancock?*)

3. Say, "Now let's look at the quiz results." Ask:
   - What was the book level of *Will You Sign Here, John Hancock?* (4.1)
   - How many questions did Jeremy get correct? (9 out of 10)
   - How many points did he earn on this book? (.9)
   - Is *Will You Sign Here, John Hancock?* a fiction or nonfiction book? (fiction)

4. Explain that the third section on the TOPS Report gives information about the student's progress so far in the marking period. Point out that "100% of MP-3" means that 100 percent, or all, of the marking period has passed. Have students look at the marking period results and compare them with Jeremy's marking period goals. Ask,
   - What is Jeremy's average book level? (4.0) What was his book-level goal? (4.1)
   - What is Jeremy's average percent correct? (78.2) Is that higher or lower than his marking period goal? (lower)
   - How many points has Jeremy earned? (24.2) What was his goal? (29.0)

5. Explain that students can quickly see if they are on track for meeting their point goal by comparing the number given in parentheses as "% of goal" with the percent of the marking period that has passed. Note that 100 percent of Jeremy's marking period has passed, but he has earned only 83.4 percent of his point goal.

6. Point out that the last two sections on the form track Jeremy's progress from the beginning of the school year and tell his certification level.

7. Tell students that you expect them to show you the TOPS Report as soon as they have taken a quiz. Ask them to highlight or circle the score on the quiz they just took as well as their average percent correct for the marking period. Tell students that seeing this helps you both monitor reading practice and, of course, celebrate success.

Status of the Class Follow-Up

As you take the Status of the Class, ask:
- Do you have a TOPS Report to show me?
- Let's look at your latest TOPS Report. Do you see any problems?
- How are you doing toward your goals?
- What do you think your next book should be?

Added Practice

- Send TOPS Reports home with students to keep parents informed about their children's reading progress. You may want to require that parents sign and return the reports to confirm that they have seen them.
- Keep hard copies of students' TOPS Reports on file so that you have a running record of students' progress available if necessary.

Using the Student Reading Log

About Using Reading Logs

Student reading logs enable you and your students to keep track of their daily reading practice. Examples are shown below. Blank forms appear on pages 94–95; blank forms also can be printed out from the Accelerated Reader software, version 5.0 and higher. On this form, students record their ZPD range (see the lesson on pages 7–9), the name of the book they are currently reading, its reading level and point value, whether the book is fiction or nonfiction, the number of pages read each day, and, when they finish the book, their score on the Accelerated Reader Reading Practice quiz.

The student reading log is a key component of Reading Renaissance because it enables you to monitor closely your students' reading. In addition, it's a "ticket" to take a quiz—students can't take a quiz unless you see the book listed on the log. In many classrooms, the log also serves as a library pass.

Objective

To help students use the student reading log to keep track of daily reading practice

Materials

A blank copy of the student reading log for each student (page 94); your current Read To book, such as *Call Me Ahnighito*, by Pam Conrad (4.4); Optional materials: An overhead projector and a transparency of the student reading log

Student Reading Log

Student Name: Jamie Sutherland   ZPD Range: 4.9–7.5

Title	Book Rdg. Level	Pts.	F/NF	Date	Pages Read in Class Begin-End	Pages Read out of Class Begin-End	% Correct	Teacher's Initials and Notes
The Mozart Season	7.3	14	F	10/12	1–16	17–33		SR
				10/13	34–51	52–63		SR
				10/15	64–76			SR
				10/16	77–92	93–101		SR
				10/20	102–120	121–136		SR
				10/21	137–150	151–162		SR
				10/22	163–172	173–186		SR
				10/23	187–199	200–216		SR

Primary Student Reading Log

Student Name: Andy Mews   ZPD: Read To 2.5–3.0 Read With 2.0–3.0 Read Ind. 1.0–1.5

		Home Use			Initial One			School Use		
Date	Quiz No.	Title	Author	Book Rdg. Level	Read To	Read With	Read Ind.	Monitor's Initials	% Correct	Teacher's Notes
4/10	7334	Mouse Tales	Arnold Lobel	2.5	✓			CM	100%	Good work, Andy!
4/10	7269	Good Morning Chick	Ginsberg	2.6	✓			CM	100%	I like this book, too.
4/10	7205	Babar's Picnic	Brunhoff	1.3			✓	CM	100%	WOW!
4/11	7388	Penrod Again	Christian	3.1		✓		CM	80%	Great job with this harder book.
4/13	5538	Ronald Morgan Goes to Bat	Gift	1.5			✓	CM	80%	Hooray! Who else in

Lesson

1. Ask, "How many of you play an instrument or participate in a sport? Do you have to keep track of your practice time? How do you do it?" Briefly discuss students' responses.

2. Hold up the student reading log. Tell students that the student reading log is a way to keep track of another important kind of practice—their reading practice. Explain that the student reading log has two important functions:
   - It gives them and you a way to track how much reading they are doing (in number of pages per day).
   - It provides a place to record their ZPD to make sure that the books they are reading are on the appropriate level.

3. Tell students that their student reading logs also are their "tickets" to taking Reading Practice quizzes. Explain that they will not be able to take a quiz on a book until you have seen on the log that they have completed the book.

4. Point to each section of the student reading log as you explain the procedure for completing the following:
   - ZPD Range: Record your *own* ZPD range in this space. (See pages 7–9.)
   - TITLE: Write the title of your independent reading book.
   - BOOK RDG. LEVEL: Write the reading level of the book. This level can be found on the book's label.
   - PTS: Write the point value of the book, which is also shown on the label.
   - F/NF: Write whether the book is a fiction or nonfiction book.
   - DATE: Write today's date. In general, there should be an entry for each day.
   - PAGES READ IN CLASS: Record the numbers of the first and last pages read independently in class.
   - PAGES READ OUT OF CLASS: Record the numbers of the first and last pages read outside of class.
   - % CORRECT: Complete this section only after you have finished reading a book and have taken the Reading Practice quiz on it.
   - INITIALS AND COMMENTS: I will initial—and sometimes make comments on—your student reading log each day during Status of the Class.

5. Using your current Read To book as an example, lead students in filling out the form for a hypothetical student.

6. Tell students, "I will check your reading logs when I come around to take the Status of the Class during reading time. Be sure to have your log filled out and open on your desk at the beginning of the period." Explain that as you check reading logs, you will talk to students not only about how many pages they've read but also about whether they are enjoying and understanding what they read.

Status of the Class Follow-Up

As you take the Status of the Class, ask:
- Let's look at your student reading log. Do you see any patterns here? It looks like you were able to read a lot (or not very much) during these days. Why was that?
- You've been going through the books at this level pretty quickly and scoring very well on quizzes. What do you think about trying some more challenging books?
- Good job! It looks like you're ready to take the quiz!
- Forty percent on a quiz tells me there's a problem here. What do you think was the problem? Where do you think you should go from here?
- Great job on the quiz! What do you want to read next?

Added Practice

- Encourage students to check their own logs before they show them to you and take a quiz.
- Use student reading logs as part of a library pass system so that the media specialist is aware of each student's ZPD and reading patterns when assisting with book selection.

Setting Goals

About Setting Goals

Goal setting is highly motivating for students. It also individualizes reading practice, encourages self-directed learning, and results in greater skill development. We recommend the following sequence for setting goals with established readers:

- First marking period: *You* pencil in each student's goals and then discuss the goals with the student.
- Second marking period: *You and the student* meet and pencil in the student's goals together.
- Third and subsequent marking periods: *The student* sets his own goals and obtains your approval. You serve as an advisor.

The following lesson is an introduction to goal setting and covers three goals—book-level goal, point goal, and minimum average percent correct. It does not cover certification or other goals. For information on certification, see the *Teacher's Handbook 3-5*. Other goals may include anything you and your students consider important in reading, for example, reading books in certain genres or by certain authors, bringing reading books and student reading logs to class each day, or reading for a designated amount of time at home. You may wish to teach additional lessons in these areas as you and your students become familiar with the goal-setting process.

To set reasonable reading goals, you must begin with an initial zone of proximal development (ZPD) for each student. See the lesson on pages 7–9 for more information on estimating initial ZPDs. Then ask yourself the following question: Does this student need to be successful or to be challenged? If the student needs success, think in terms of goals that she can definitely achieve. If the student needs challenge, encourage her to take on more ambitious goals.

Above all, remember that goal setting is a matter of balance and judgment, not hard-and-fast rule. Listen to your instincts as you work with students and the information from Accelerated Reader. Ask yourself, "What goals will encourage this student to read more?" The answer will help you make sure that the goals you and the student set are realistic but challenging.

Reproducible versions of the Goal-Setting Chart and the Student Reading Plan are on pages 96 and 98. You can also print blank forms using Accelerated Reader 5.0 or higher.

Objective To introduce students to setting goals in reading and using the Student Reading Plan

Materials A copy of a blank Student Reading Plan and the Goal-Setting Chart for each student (pages 96 and 98); Optional materials: An overhead projector and transparencies of the Student Reading Plan and Goal-Setting Chart

Lesson
1. Ask, "Have you ever set a goal for yourself? What was it?" If necessary, suggest possible goals that students might set, for example, getting their homework done before their favorite TV show, saving money for a new CD, or scoring a goal in the next soccer game. Tell students, "Having a goal makes you want to try your best. And when you reach your goal, how do you feel? Great!"

2. Ask students to discuss what makes good goals. Be sure that the discussion includes the following points:
   - Good goals should be challenging but achievable.
   - Good goals should be geared toward the individual.

3. Direct students' attention to the Student Reading Plan. Tell students that you and they will be using this plan to set their reading goals. Point out the different sections of the plan as you discuss each of the following with students:
   - ZPD: Your zone of proximal development, or ZPD, is the range of book levels that is not too hard nor too easy for you to read. (See the lesson on pages 7–9 for more information.)
   - BOOK-LEVEL GOAL: "Book level" refers to the grade-level difficulty of different books. As you practice reading and become a better reader, you'll be able to read higher level books. For example, if you are reading books that have an average difficulty of 4.1, you might set a goal of reading books that average 4.2 by the end of the next marking period. The books in our library have a label that tells you what the book level is.
   - POINT GOAL: "Points" are a way of measuring the reading practice you are doing. The more reading practice you do, the greater number of points you will earn. The Goal-Setting Chart helps us estimate how many points someone with your ZPD range should aim for at first. After that, your point goal will be based on what will help you read more.
   - MINIMUM AVERAGE % CORRECT: If you are reading books that are at the right level for you, you will do well on the Reading Practice quizzes. So the average percent correct that I expect is the same for everyone—85 percent or higher.

4. Have students help you fill out a Student Reading Plan for a hypothetical student—perhaps one named Rabid Reader. Identify the student's ZPD—say, 4.0—and then fill in a book-level goal, point goal (using the Goal-Setting Chart as a guideline), and minimum average percent correct.
5. Tell students that you will be setting goals with them individually. Ask them to look over the Student Reading Plan and take some time before you meet to think about what goals would be good for them to set for themselves.

Status of the Class Follow-Up

Use Status of the Class every two or three weeks to review individual students' goals and adjust them as necessary. (See the *Teacher's Handbook 3-5* for more information.) During individual goal-setting conferences, ask:
- How do you feel your reading is going?
- Let's look at the goals we've set. Do you think you can reach them?
- Are you having difficulty in any area?
- Do you think you're ready for more challenge? In what way?
- What would help you reach your goals?

Added Practice

- At the end of each marking period, give students copies of their Student Record Reports. Ask students to write down five observations about their progress, for example:
  – Which goals did you meet?
  – Which goals do you think need to be adjusted?
  – Did anything prevent you from meeting your goals? What was it?
- Introduce the Reader Certification system (see the *Teacher's Handbook 3-5* for more information) and help students set certification goals.
- Encourage small groups of students to brainstorm a list of ideas for the section on "Other Goals." Have the groups share their ideas with the class. Then have each student choose one "Other Goal" to set for the marking period.

Author's Purpose

Objective To help students understand that authors often write for the purpose of informing, entertaining, or persuading their readers

Materials Several books (fiction and nonfiction) that loosely share a topic but demonstrate distinct and different purposes for writing, such as *The Earth* (4.6) by Cynthia Pratt Nicolson (to inform); *Earth to Matthew* (4.1) by Paula Danzinger (to entertain); and *Earthwise At School* (5.0) by Linda Lowery and Marybeth Lorbiecki (to persuade). You may also want to choose a book that demonstrates two equally important purposes such as *The Magic School Bus Inside the Earth* (3.6) by Joanna Cole (to inform and to entertain).

Lesson

1. Hold up the books that you have chosen. Ask students, "What do all of these books have in common?" (They all have the word *earth* in their title.)

2. Now hold up the book you have chosen that demonstrates the author's intent to inform. Read a few passages from this book to students and ask, "Why do you think the author wrote this book?" Possible responses for *The Earth* might be:
   - To teach us about the earth
   - To provide facts about the earth
   - To help us conduct experiments or make projects

   Tell students that authors often write books or articles to give us information—or to inform us about specific topics.

3. Next, read a passage from your selection intended to demonstrate that writers can choose to entertain readers. Choose a passage that is funny or suspenseful, rather than one in which the author is describing or explaining something. For instance, you might read this passage from *Earth to Matthew*:

   > "Over the teeth and over the gums, look out stomach, here it comes." Matthew wolfs down his fourth cupcake and takes a swig of soda.
   >
   > There's marshmallow icing across his upper lip.
   >
   > Joshua Jackson, his best friend, reaches for a handful of chocolate chip cookies. "I can't believe that you're not eating more of these. . . ."
   >
   > Holding open his backpack, Matthew shows that he has taken about a dozen of them.

   Ask, "Why do you think the author wrote this book?" Possible answers might be:
   - To make us laugh
   - To tell a great story
   - To keep us turning the pages

   Point out that many authors write books to entertain their audience.

4. Tell students that you are going to read a passage from a third book and that although it might seem as if the author's goal is to inform the reader, the author has a slightly different (or additional) purpose in mind. Then read a passage that clearly demonstrates the author's intention to persuade. Here is an example from *Earthwise at School*:

   > [T]he exhaust from cars, trucks, and planes is one of the greatest causes of air pollution. So what can you do about that? Plenty! Walk, skateboard, bike, in-line skate, or roller-skate to places. Share car rides. Take buses, subways, and trains. Make it a game with your friends and family to see how little you can use the car.

   Again, ask: "Why do you think the author wrote this book?" (to convince us to take better care of the earth). Point out that authors sometimes write a book or an article to persuade readers to do something, or to think about a topic in a certain way.

5. Write the three purposes on the chalkboard: to inform, to entertain, and to persuade. Explain that while some authors may have only one purpose for writing a piece, many authors write for more than one purpose. Hold up *The Magic School Bus Inside the Earth*, and ask, "What parts of this book are meant to entertain you? What parts are meant to inform you?"

6. Ask students to consider the author's purpose or purposes when they are reading their own selections. Tell them that knowing the author's purpose can help them to understand better and match the pace of their reading to the reading material. For instance, if the author's purpose is to inform, they might read the passage more slowly to understand the information. If the author's purpose is to persuade they might ask themselves, "Do I agree with the author?"

Status of the Class Follow-Up

As you take the Status of the Class, ask:
- Why do you think the author wrote this book?
- Does knowing the author's purpose help you understand what you are reading? If so, in what ways?
- How would changing the author's purpose change the way in which the book was written?

Added Practice

- Provide students with a topic and ask them to write three book titles that demonstrate different authors' purposes. For instance, given the topic of *running*, students might come up with:
  - *How to Increase Your Running Time*
  - *Running From Googly Monsters*
  - *Run Every Day!*
- Create a Venn diagram with three overlapping circles on a bulletin board. Have students write the titles of favorite books on the diagram indicating whether the author had a single, double, or triple purpose for writing the book.

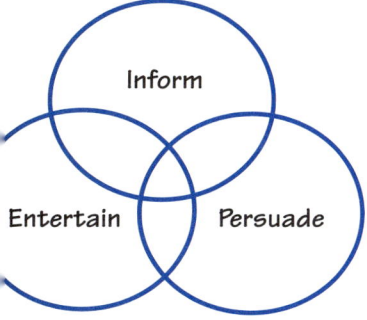

Classifying and Categorizing

Objective To help students to make associations and distinctions in order to classify words

Materials Any nonfiction book you have recently read to students or could read in one sitting, such as *The Honey Makers* by Gail Gibbons (4.8)

Lesson
1. Choose words from your nonfiction selection that could easily fit under more than one heading. Add random words that do not relate to the possible headings. Write the list of words on the chalkboard. The list from *The Honey Makers* might look like this, with *sneaker, castle, snow, dribble,* and *ball* added randomly:

court	royal	dribble
sneaker	castle	wax
queen	chamber	dance
guard	snow	ball

2. Ask students: "Do you see any way of classifying some of these words into smaller groups?" Remind students that to classify words is to arrange them in groups according to what they have in common. Have students provide a heading for their lists. Here are two possible ways that students might arrange some of the words:

Fairy Tale Words	Basketball
court	court
queen	sneaker
royal	dribble
chamber	guard
ball	ball

3. If students do not suggest a heading from the nonfiction book you selected, suggest that heading now. Or read the book and ask students to suggest a new heading when you are finished. For *The Honey Makers*, students might suggest this heading:

   <u>Words Having to Do With Bee Hives</u>

court	dance	guard
queen	wax	
royal	chamber	

4. Tell students that many books, and nonfiction books in particular, contain words that describe a subject. Thinking about those words as a group and attaching a name to them will help them understand the meanings of specific words and the ideas of the book in general.

Status of the Class Follow-Up

As you take the Status of the Class, ask:
- List five interesting words from your book. Can you think of headings that you could use to classify some of the words?
- Do you think you might run into other words that fall under that classification? Why or why not?
- Have you ever read a story containing words that could only be found in that story? (Examples of fiction that have invented vocabulary are the Harry Potter Books by J.K. Rowling, *Frindle* by Andrew Clements, or *Walk Two Moons* by Sharon Creech.) What are some different ways you might classify those words?

Added Practice

- Begin with a single word and have students make a web that illustrates the many categories that the word could belong to. For instance, the word *box* might generate all of these categories: *Sports, Containers, Rhymes With Fox, Words With X, Things You Might Find in a Garage*.
- The next time you read a nonfiction book, invite students to choose interesting words from that book and see how many ways they can classify the words to make new category lists.
- Have students use words from their independent reading books to make word webs like the one shown below.

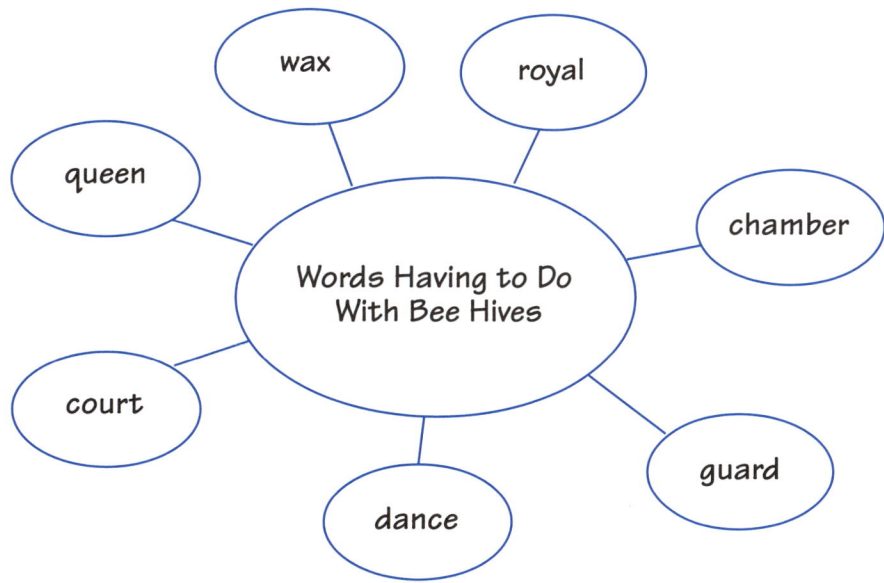

Compare and Contrast

Objective To help students compare and contrast two trickster tales, thereby increasing their ability to tell how two or more stories are similar and different

Materials Two trickster tales from different cultures such as *Coyote and the Laughing Butterflies* by Harriet Taylor (4.2) and *Aunt Nancy and Old Man Trouble* by Phyllis Root (4.2)

Lesson

1. Remind students that they often compare and contrast information in their own lives. For instance, whenever they choose between two or more foods on a menu or activities in an afterschool program, they are using their skills of comparing and contrasting.

2. Read or review two brief trickster tales with students. Tell students that tricksters are characters that often appear in folktales—stories that have been handed down from generation to generation by storytellers. Sometimes the tricksters fool other characters, and sometimes the tricksters get fooled themselves, but there is always a good deal of mischief and confusion when a trickster is around.

3. Create a three-column chart on the chalkboard. On the far left-hand side write the name of one book. On the far right-hand side, write the name of the other. In the center, write the word *both*.

4. Ask students to compare the two stories. Remind them to *compare* means to determine how two or more things are alike and how they are different. A chart comparing *Coyote and the Laughing Butterflies* and *Aunt Nancy and Old Man Trouble* might look something like this:

Coyote	Both	Aunt Nancy
Coyote is fooled by the butterflies.	Neither Coyote nor Old Man Trouble know they're being fooled.	Old Man Trouble is fooled by Aunt Nancy's words.

5. After you have completed the chart, take a moment to focus on the ways in which these two books differ. Tell students that looking at the differences between the two books is to *contrast* them.

6. Tell students that comparing and contrasting stories they've read will help them understand more about what the stories really mean.

Status of the Class Follow-Up

As you take the Status of the Class, ask:
- Does the book you are reading now remind you of any other books you have read?
- How are the books the same? How are they different?
- In what ways might comparing and contrasting two different books be useful?

Added Practice

- Have students use the three-column comparison chart shown on page 22 to compare and contrast two books of a different genre. You could compare two fairy tales, pourquoi tales, or two stories that have the same theme. Comparing two nonfiction books on the same topic would help students to recognize that authors often make different choices when writing about the same information.
- Compare and contrast several versions of the same story with the class. For instance, there are *Cinderella* stories from almost every culture. Or compare and contrast two fairy tales written from two separate points of view. For instance, you could compare *The Three Little Pigs* with *The True Story of the Three Little Pigs* by Jon Scieszka (3.0), which tells the traditional story from the Wolf's point of view.

Drawing Conclusions

Objective To help students use the skill of drawing conclusions or making inferences to improve comprehension

Materials Any story or novel you have recently read to students, such as *Ella Enchanted* by Gail Carson Levine (4.6)

Lesson

1. Present the following scenario:

    It's your birthday. The teacher asks you to take a note to the principal's office at the end of the day. When you return to your classroom, the lights are off and there appears to be no one there. You do notice that there is a stack of paper cups on one desk. What is your conclusion? (Possible answer: The class is throwing you a surprise party.)

2. Tell students that they *draw conclusions* every day. Add that they also draw conclusions—or, as it's sometimes called, *make inferences*—every time they read a book or hear a story. Ask a volunteer to give a brief synopsis of the book you are reading aloud. Then read a passage from the story that requires readers to draw conclusions about a character's actions or words. For instance, you might use this example of when Ella met Hattie, her soon-to-be stepsister, in Ella's home for the very first time in *Ella Enchanted*:

    > Hattie surveyed the room. "This is a fine hall, almost as fine as the palace where I'm going to live someday. Our mother, Dame Olga, says your father is very rich. She says he can make money out of anything." . . .She opened the wardrobe in Mother's room and, before I could stop her, ran her hands over Mother's gowns. When we got back to the hall she announced, "Forty-two windows and a fireplace in every room. The windows must have cost a trunkful of gold KJs."

3. Ask, "What conclusions can you draw about Hattie from this selection?" List students' responses on the board. Possible responses include:

    - **She is interested in money and fine things.**
    - **Her mother thinks about money and how much money Ella's father has.**
    - **She doesn't pay much attention to Ella.**

4. Ask students, "How did you know these things about Hattie when the author didn't come right out and tell you?" Guide students to understand that they make inferences by:
    - Paying attention to the character's appearance, conversation, and tone of voice.
    - Noting important actions or events.

- Thinking about the details.
- Applying information you've gathered and what you already know from your own experiences.

5. Remind students that if they draw conclusions as they read, they will be able to better understand characters and their actions in stories.

Status of the Class Follow-Up

As you take the Status of the Class, ask:

- What is the main character in your book like? What actions or details support your conclusions?
- What else do you know that lead you to draw that conclusion?
- Is your conclusion the only reasonable conclusion? What other conclusion could someone draw? Has someone in the book come to a different conclusion about this character?

Added Practice

- Suggest that pairs of students read copies of the same book and meet periodically to "think aloud." Model this strategy by reading a section of the text that raises questions and then making inferences out loud. For instance, you might read this passage from *Ella Enchanted*:

    "Why did you listen to him?" Char asked. . . .

    I had to answer, somehow. "His eyes," I lied.

  Then share your thoughts, drawing a conclusion: "I think that Ella didn't want to lie. She likes Prince Char, but she must be careful not to tell her curse. Whoever knows about the curse has power over her." Encourage students to share their conclusions in the same way.

- Post a photograph, magazine picture, or painting that depicts a scene. Invite students to draw conclusions about what is happening in the scene and the personalities of the people who are participating along with information or experiences to support their conclusions.

- Ask students to keep a literature dialogue journal. Encourage them to write to you, sharing their reactions to books and particularly to the development of characters. Write back to students and include questions that help them to focus on their observations and prior knowledge to draw conclusions.

Fact and Opinion

Objective To help students differentiate between statements of fact and statements of opinion

Materials Any nonfiction book you have recently read to students, such as *Ellis Island* by Patricia Ryon Quiri (4.9)

Lesson

1. On the chalkboard, write two statements from or related to a current event or nonfiction book that you are reading to the class. One sentence should be a statement of fact and the other a statement of opinion, for example:

   The very first immigrant to be registered at the new immigration center was an Irish girl named Annie Moore.

   Going to a new country is exciting.

2. Tell students that a statement of fact can be proven true or false, whereas statements of opinion cannot be proven.

3. Point to the first statement on the board and ask, "Is this a statement of fact or opinion?" (fact). Ask students how they know (because the information can be checked) and how the information could be checked.

4. Point to the second statement on the board and ask, "Is this a statement of fact or opinion? Ask how students know (it can't be proven true or false). Ask, "If you agreed with this statement, would that make it a fact?" Point out that statements of opinion represent what someone thinks, and that although the opinion may be commonly accepted, it is still a statement of opinion.

5. Choose several more statements from your book or article and ask students to tell you if the sentences are statements of opinion or fact. After each response ask, "Can this information be proven?" (You may come across sentences that combine fact and opinion. Go ahead and point this out.)

6. Tell students to look for statements of fact or opinion in their books and be prepared to tell you why they came to their conclusions.

Status of the Class Follow-Up

As you take the Status of the Class, ask:
- Can you find a statement of fact or opinion in your book?
- Why do you think that it is a statement of fact or opinion?
- How might you prove this statement true or false?

Added Practice

- Encourage students to collect statements of fact or opinion. Each day, invite several students to present the class with a statement. Classmates must say whether the statement is fact or opinion and why. When appropriate, challenge students to find out whether a statement of fact is correct or incorrect.
- Have students write a brief paragraph about a nonfiction topic of interest. Ask them to include at least one statement of fact and one statement of opinion in their essay.

Main Idea and Details

Objective To help students identify the main idea and supporting details of a piece of writing

Materials Any nonfiction book related to a current theme of study, such as *What Happened to the Dinosaurs?* by Franklyn M. Branley (4.3); brief announcement with a stated main idea about an upcoming activity from a newspaper or school newsletter

Lesson

1. Read aloud the announcement. Ask:
   - What event is this announcement about? (For example, the Fall Festival.)
   - What is the most important idea about the event? (The Fall Festival will be on October 22.)

2. Write the following on the board:

   <u>Topic:</u> What or who am I reading about?
   <u>Main Idea:</u> What is the most important idea about this topic?

   Remind students that the main idea of a selection is sometimes given in a sentence telling the most important idea about the topic.

3. Tell students that sometimes the main idea is stated in a selection, as it was in the announcement. Explain that often, however, the main idea is not stated and they must figure it out by thinking about what one idea the important details in the selection all tell about.

4. Read aloud a selection from your nonfiction book. Make sure that the selection contains a strong main idea that is not stated directly, such as this one from *What Happened to the Dinosaurs*.

   > Sixty-five million years ago, thousands of comets may have crashed into the Earth. That would have produced a lot of heat. Wildfires would have swept through forests and swamps. Plants would have burned up, and dinosaurs would have, too. Only small animals that could dig into the ground would have escaped.
   >
   > After the fire had burned out, the theory says, the air was heavy with soot, ash, and dust. There was so much, the sun could not shine through. Earth got colder and colder. Many plants that had survived the fire could not grow. There was little food for any dinosaurs that might have survived the Earth fire. So they starved.

5. Draw the following diagram on the board.

Comets may have crashed into the Earth.   **MAIN IDEA: Comets may have destroyed the dinosaurs.**   Fires may have killed the dinosaurs.

6. Ask students to help you list some supporting pieces of information, or *details*, from the paragraph. Record the details on the spokes of the diagram. Ask, "What *one* main idea do all these details tell about?" (how comets may have destroyed the dinosaurs). Write the main idea in the circle.

7. Tell students that thinking about the main idea will help them understand and remember what they read. Remind them of these strategies for finding the main idea:
   - Ask yourself, "What or who am I reading about? What is the most important idea about this topic?"
   - If you can't find a sentence that tells the main idea, think about the details in the selection. Ask, "What important idea do all these details tell about?"
   - Ask, "Do most of the details support the main idea?"

Status of the Class Follow-Up

As you take the Status of the Class, ask:
- Who or what are you reading about?
- What is the main idea of the part you are currently reading?
- How did you figure out what the main idea was?
- What are some important details that tell about the main idea?

Added Practice

- Give students short newspaper articles with the headlines cut off. Ask them to write a headline that clearly states the main idea of each article.
- Post pictures relating to a current theme of study. On index cards, have students write the main idea of what is happening in the picture and three or four supporting details. Post the index cards next to the pictures.

Making Generalizations

Objective To help students use clue words to recognize a generalization in text

Materials Any nonfiction book you have recently read to students, such as *If You Traveled on the Underground Railroad* by Ellen Levine (4.9)

Lesson
1. Write the following question on the board:

   Would you rather have ice cream or egg custard for dessert?

   Poll the students and tally their responses to this question. Then use the data to write a generalization. For example:

   Most kids in our class prefer ice cream over egg custard for dessert.

2. Tell students that a *generalization* is a general rule drawn from looking at facts or events. Encourage them to make their own generalizations about life in your classroom. Use generalizations such as these to get them started:
   - We usually become quiet when we hear the intercom.
   - Everyone in our class loves independent reading time.
   - We always pick up after ourselves.

3. Tell students that authors also make generalizations. Help them to understand that authors research and collect facts to make generalizations about the subjects they are writing about. Read a few generalizations from your current Read To book, such as these from *If You Traveled on the Underground Railroad*:
   - "Everyone was afraid of being sold to owners who lived in Georgia and Alabama."
   - "Most runaway slaves went to the northern states."
   - "[Runaway slaves] usually had a password or special signal to look out for."

4. Explain that clue words such as *everyone* or *everybody*, *all*, *none*, *most*, *usually*, and *always* often tell us that the author has made a generalization. Post the clue words on the board and ask students to listen for a generalization while you read a passage aloud. Have students determine which sentence contains a generalization. In the following paragraph, the generalization is underlined:

   > "Some slave women would go on board a ship carrying clean, ironed shirts. <u>Everybody thought they were bringing laundry to the sailors</u>. Once on board, they hid and sailed to a northern port."

5. Tell students that recognizing generalizations that authors make will help them understand what they read. Ask students to watch for generalizations as they read and to notice which clue words helped them to identify the generalizations.

Status of the Class Follow-Up

As you take the Status of the Class, ask:
- Have you found any generalizations in your book?
- What clue words helped you to find a generalization?
- Why do you think the author made a generalization? What point was the author trying to make?

Added Practice

- Students can search the newspaper for generalizations of current events. Suggest that they underline the clues words that helped them to identify the generalization.
- Help students to recognize their own use of generalizations. Chances are they've once said something along the lines of, "But Mom, all of the kids in my class have electronic games." Suggest that students begin a bulletin board of the generalizations they catch themselves and others using.

Multiple Causes and Effects

Objective To help students identify cause and effect relationships with multiple causes and/or multiple effects

Materials Any book you have recently read to students, such as *Good Times on Grandfather Mountain* by Jacqueline Briggs Martin (4.0)

Lesson

1. Write the words "School was called off!" in a circle on the board. Ask students, "What would you do if the principal called off school today?" As children brainstorm possible results, write them in smaller circles below the words "School was called off!" Draw arrows from the cause (school was called off) to the effects (what students would do).

2. Remind students that "why something happened" (school is called off) is called the *cause* and "what happened" (events listed) are called the *effects*. Point out that sometimes one cause can have many effects—in real life and in stories.

3. Demonstrate that a cause can have multiple effects in books by asking questions from your Read To book. For example, ask, "In *Good Times on Grandfather Mountain*, what happened when Washburn played his fiddle?" Student answers might include:
   - Washburn's neighbors came running to play music and dance.
   - The cow, the pig, and the chickens returned.
   - Everyone pitched in and rebuilt Washburn's cabin.

4. Tell students that just as one cause can have many effects, one effect can have many causes. Bring students back to your diagram on the chalkboard. Ask, "Why might the principal have called off school?" Record student responses in circles above the statement "School was called off!" with arrows pointing to the effect.

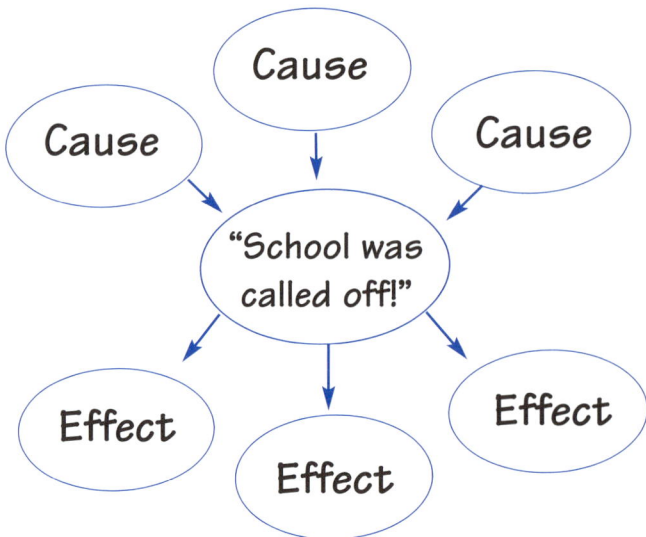

5. Use your Read To book to reinforce the concept that one effect can have many causes. Ask, "Why did Washburn do nothing more than sit on his front porch and play his fiddle?" Possible student responses might be:
- He had wood in the pile.
- There was no cow to milk.
- There was no pig to feed.
- There were no eggs to find.
- There were no beans to pick.
- There was no roof to fix.

6. Ask students to look for cause and effect relationships as they read their books. Remind them to ask themselves "What happened?" to find the effect(s) and "Why did it happen?" to find the cause(s).

Status of the Class Follow-Up

As you take the Status of the Class, ask:
- What just happened in the story you are reading?
- Why did it happen?
- Could there be more than one cause of that event?
- Could there be more than one effect or result of that event?

Added Practice

- Challenge students to come up with a "what if" statement: What if you could see behind walls? What if you could get your driver's license at the age of ten? What if you grew younger instead of older? Then have them create their own diagram with possible causes and effects.
- Have each student think of a cause and write a list of multiple effects. Then invite students to read their lists aloud while others suggest possible causes. For instance one student might read: "ice-cream melted instantly, lakes dried up, the grass turned brown." The cause? A heat wave.

Predicting Outcomes

Objective To help students develop strategies for predicting outcomes

Materials *The Fortune-Tellers* by Lloyd Alexander (4.6), or another fiction or nonfiction book that can be read in one sitting

Lesson
1. Present students with the following scenario:
   > You look out the window and see that the sky has grown dark with heavy clouds. A stiff wind is rustling the leaves of the trees. In the distance, you hear the faint rumble of thunder. What do you predict is going to happen?

2. Tell students that a *prediction* is a statement that tells what might happen or come next. Ask students what information they used to predict that it might rain. Point out that they used sensory clues—things that could be heard or seen—as well as their own experience with rainstorms to predict what would happen. Explain that good readers continually make and adjust predictions as they read.

3. Begin reading *The Fortune-Tellers*. Stop reading after the cloth merchant's wife mistakes the carpenter for the fortune-teller. Ask, "What do you think the carpenter will do now?"

4. Draw the following chart on the board. List students' predictions in the column labeled "Prediction." Help students fill in the other two columns by asking questions such as:
   - What in the story makes you think the carpenter will do that?
   - Have you ever been mistaken for someone else? What did you do?
   - If you were the carpenter, what would you do?

Prediction	What I know from the story	What I know from my own experience

5. Read on, pausing after the sentence, "At a loss for what else to do, he recalled what the fortune-teller had told him." Ask, "Now what do you think the carpenter will do? Do you have a new prediction?" Add any new predictions and support to the chart.

6. Finish reading the book. Ask, "Did the carpenter do what you predicted he would?" Tell students that making and, if necessary, changing predictions as they read will make their reading more interesting and enjoyable.

Status of the Class Follow-Up

As you take the Status of the Class, ask:
- What is this book about?
- What do you predict will happen next? (for fiction)
- What do you predict you will learn about next? (for nonfiction)
- What do you know from the story or your own experience that supports your prediction?

Added Practice

- Have students fold sheets of paper or journal pages in half to make two columns. Have them label the columns "Predictions" and "Support." As students read, have them write their predictions and support from the text and their own experience in the appropriate columns.
- Suggest that students use small index cards as prediction bookmarks. After they've read the first few pages or the first chapter of a book, have them record their predictions about the book on the card. For fiction books, have them write what they think will happen in the story. For nonfiction books, have them write what they might learn from the book. Suggest that students use the cards as bookmarks. Then, as they read, they can adjust their predictions or write new predictions as their knowledge of the book increases.

Previewing and Setting a Purpose

Objective To help students preview a piece of writing and set a purpose for reading

Materials Any nonfiction book related to a current theme of study, such as *An Island Scrapbook* by Virginia Wright-Frierson (4.9)

Lesson

1. Ask students to imagine they are reading the menu at a fast-food restaurant. Say, "You might have different reasons for reading that menu. Perhaps you are choosing what you want to have for lunch. Or maybe you just came in for a cold drink and want to see how much it costs. Or perhaps you're just reading it to pass the time while you wait for your order." Ask questions that lead students to think about how their different purposes for reading the menu would affect how they read the menu. For example:
   - If you just came in for a cold drink, would you read the whole menu?
   - If you were trying to decide what to order, what information would you look for?
   - If you were reading the menu just to pass the time, would you read it quickly or at a slow rate? Why?

2. Tell students that good readers always have a purpose in mind when they read. Hold up a book from the classroom library and ask, "What are some purposes you might have for reading this book?" List students' responses on the board. Responses might include:

   - **For entertainment**
   - **To find out more information about a subject**
   - **To learn how to do something**

3. Tell students that the more specific their purpose for reading is, the more enjoyment and use they will get out of their reading. Say, "One way you can figure out your specific purpose for reading something is by taking some time to browse through or *preview* a book before you begin to read it." Hold up a book that is related to a current theme of study, such as *An Island Scrapbook*. Model asking yourself questions to establish a purpose for reading or make your purpose more specific. For example: I want to find out more information about ocean environments. As I look this book over, I ask myself, "Does this book tell about ocean environments? What specific information does this book contain? What should I pay attention to in this book?"

4. Turn to a graphic element in the book, such as the diagram in *An Island Scrapbook* that shows the dangers to sea turtles. Continue to model self-questioning: I've seen from the title, covers, and illustrations that this book will suit my purpose for finding information about the ocean. Now I want to know what information it will give me. When I look at this diagram, I ask myself, "What do I know about sea turtles? What do I want to know?"

5. Draw a K-W-L chart on the board, such as the one shown below, to help students visualize their thinking process:

What I Know	What I Want to Know	What I Learned
Sea turtles live in the ocean.	Why are sea turtles in danger?	

6. Have students look at the information in the "What I Know" column. Ask, "If you were to sort this information into groups of larger ideas, what categories might you use?" (what it looks like, which animals live there, and so on)

7. Tell students, "During Status of the Class, I'll be asking each of you to tell me your purpose in reading your book and to show me how you would preview your book with that purpose in mind."

Status of the Class Follow-Up

As you take the Status of the Class, ask:
- What is your purpose for reading this book?
- Show me what you might do to preview this book. What kind of information would you look for?
- If you had a different purpose for reading—say, for enjoyment rather than for study—would that change the way you read the book? How?

Added Practice

- Suggest that students draw a K-W-L chart on a sheet of paper. Encourage them to use the chart to record questions and information as they read. Have them fold the paper in half lengthwise and use it as a bookmark so that the chart will always be handy.
- Invite pairs or small groups of students to read the same book and discuss it in temporary "Book Clubs." Have them jot down and discuss questions that arise while previewing and reading the book.

Self-Correction Strategies

Objective To give students strategies for monitoring and self-correcting their reading

Materials Any book you are currently reading to students, such as *Outside and Inside Birds* by Sandra Markle (4.9)

Lesson

1. Tell students that even good readers sometimes run into unfamiliar words or sections of writing that they don't understand. Write a passage that contains an unfamiliar word, such as this one from *Outside and Inside Birds*:

   Next, muscles squeeze, pushing the food into the <u>gizzard</u>, where strong muscles do much the same job your teeth do when you chew your food.

2. Begin to read the sentence aloud, pausing before the word *gizzard*. Tell students, "Let's say I'm reading along, and I get stuck on this word. What can I do?" As you discuss students' suggestions, write the following strategies on the board:

   <u>Fix-Up Strategies</u>
   Slow down.
   Think about what you already know.
   Read on.
   Reread.

3. Point to the first strategy and tell students, "Sometimes readers get stuck simply because they are reading too fast. If something doesn't make sense or you run into an unfamiliar word, the first thing you should do is slow down. Then think about what you already know about the word. For example, I know that the word *gizzard* looks like another word I know—*blizzard*. By substituting the sound of *g* for *bl*, I can figure out how to pronounce the word. Now, it seems to me that I've heard that word somewhere before. Oh yes! It was at Thanksgiving. Maybe a gizzard is a part of a turkey!"

4. Point to the third strategy and say, "Sometimes you can figure out a word by skipping the word and reading to the end of the sentence." Use the sentence on the board to model the strategy. Then ask, "What clues does the rest of the sentence give you about the meaning of *gizzard*?" (that food gets ground up there)

5. Point to the fourth strategy and say, "Finally, go back and reread the paragraph that contains the sentence with the unfamiliar word. Tell students, "This paragraph tells about what happens to the food a bird swallows. I can tell from the paragraph that a *gizzard* must be a body part that breaks down the food that birds eat."
6. Tell students that using fix-up strategies like the ones listed on the board will help them figure out words, sentences, or even sections that they find confusing while they are reading.

Status of the Class Follow-Up

As you take the Status of the Class, ask:
- Have you run into a word you don't know or a confusing part while you've been reading?
- What did you do to figure out the word or the meaning?
- Have you tried using any of the fix-up strategies we talked about? Which ones?

Added Practice

- Cut hammer-shaped bookmarks from construction paper. Have students copy the four fix-up strategies mentioned in the lesson onto the bookmarks. Encourage students to refer to the strategies listed on their bookmarks whenever they get stuck on a word or are confused.
- Have pairs of students listen to each other read passages containing difficult words. Encourage students to use fix-up strategies to support each other as they try to figure out the words.
- Give students self-sticking notes so that they can mark passages or words that baffle them. During Status of the Class, use these passages to help students practice using self-correcting strategies.

Sequence

Objective To help students identify the order in which things happen in a story

Materials Any book with a straightforward sequence of events, such as *A River Ran Wild* by Lynn Cherry (4.7); large strips of tagboard, masking tape

Lesson
1. Read aloud *A River Ran Wild* or another appropriate book. As you read, write the major events on strips of tagboard. For example, events from *A River Ran Wild* might include:
   - Native people settle on the river.
   - European settlers build villages and mills.
   - Native people are driven from the land.
   - Factories dump pollutants into the river.
   - Wildlife die from the poisons.
   - Oweana and Marion decide to help the river.
   - People start a clean-up campaign.
   - Wildlife returns to the river.
2. On the board, draw a large time line, story map, or other sequencing graphic. (A river would work well for *A River Ran Wild*.) Be sure that the graphic is divided into as many sections as there are event strips.
3. Shuffle the tagboard strips and place them along the chalk tray. Ask, "What event happened first?" Ask a volunteer to tape the appropriate card in the proper section on the graphic. Follow the same procedure for the rest of the events.
4. Ask students to keep the sequence of events in mind as they read their own books. Remind them that certain clue words, such as *first*, *next*, *then*, and *last*, and phrases referring to time (*last Saturday*, *that night*) tell when things happen. Also warn students that authors do not always use clue words, and they must ultimately rely on their own ideas about what order makes sense.

Status of the Class Follow-Up

As you take the Status of the Class, ask:
- Can you tell me three (or more) events that have happened in your book so far?
- In what order did they happen?
- Did any clue words help you figure out the order? Which ones?

Added Practice

- Students can draw comic strips showing a sequence of events from a book they have read. Pairs of students who have read the same book can make comic strips, cut apart the individual frames, and challenge their partners to put the strips in order again.
- Encourage students to create sets of directions for doing simple tasks like brushing teeth, making a peanut butter sandwich, or looking up a word in the dictionary. Have them include a mistake in each set of directions. Perhaps a step is missing or out of sequence, or the list includes irrelevant information. Have students exchange lists, correct the sequence, and rewrite the directions in the proper order.

Summarizing Nonfiction

Objective To help students use the skill of summarizing to improve comprehension

Materials A brief "amazing fact" article from the newspaper or a nonfiction book, such as *Weird Animals* by Tammy Everts (4.2)

Lesson

1. Read aloud the "amazing facts" article or a paragraph or two from the nonfiction book, such as this one from *Weird Animals*:

   > The island of Komodo is part of a country called Indonesia. This island is home to an animal called the Komodo dragon. The Komodo dragon is not really a dragon, but it does look like a creature from a fairy tale. It has scaly skin and a long tail. The Komodo dragon is the largest lizard in the world. It can grow up to four meters (13 feet) long. That is longer than a car!

2. Discuss the information in the article for a few moments. Then say, "Let's suppose you go home this evening and your mom or dad says, 'Did you learn anything new in school today?' How would you tell about what we just read?"

3. Listen as a few students give summaries of the article. Then say, "Each of you just gave a *summary* of the article we just read." Explain that a summary tells the main ideas of a piece of writing. Emphasize that summaries are short—no more than a few sentences—and that they include only the most important ideas.

4. Draw the following diagram on the board.

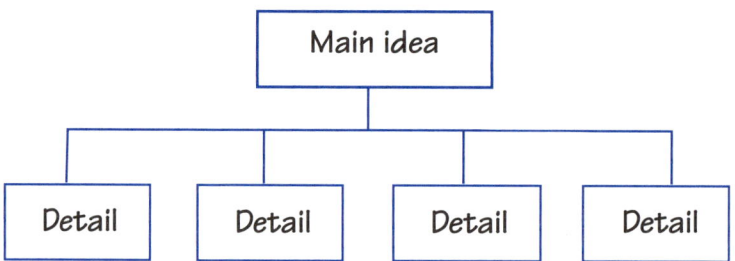

5. Ask students to help you fill in the chart. The completed chart for the paragraph about Komodo dragons might look like the following:

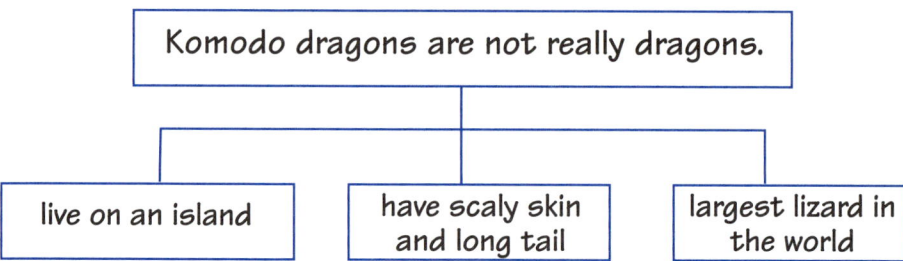

6. Use the information in the diagram to write a brief summary of the book. Review the summary and ask, "What information from the article did we leave out of the summary?" (Komodo is part of Indonesia; four meters is longer than a car.) Remind students that summaries are always short and contain only the most important information from a book or article.
7. Tell students that summarizing what they have read will help them remember and better understand their reading.

Status of the Class Follow-Up

As you take the Status of the Class, ask:
- Can you tell me in a few sentences what this book (or section of the book) is about?
- What is the main idea of this selection?
- What are some of the most important details?
- Which details did you choose to leave out of your summary? Why?

Added Practice

- Start a book recommendation card file. On index cards, students can write the titles, authors, and summaries of books they think others would like. To encourage students to be brief, have them limit the length of their summaries to one side of the index card.
- Have students complete diagrams like the one on page 42 to write "News Flashes" summarizing the main ideas of a selection.
- Create an interactive bulletin board by asking students to write summaries of their favorite books. Post the summaries and a separate list of the books' titles. Encourage students to match each title to its summary.

Text Features: Headings and Subheadings

Objective To help students use headings and subheadings to improve comprehension

Materials Any nonfiction book or textbook with headings and subheadings, such as *Pocket Pets* by Alvin and Virginia Silverstein

Lesson
1. Hold up a nonfiction book or textbook related to your current theme of study. Turn to the beginning of a chapter or section that contains a main heading and several subheadings. Ask, "What is this section about? How do you know?" Point out that informational books often have *headings* that tell what different sections of the book are about.

2. Point to the heading and ask, "What do you notice about these words? How are they different from the other words on the page?" Explain that the heading of a section usually appears in larger or darker print.

3. Tell students, "Suppose I wanted to find out what kind of information the author gives about this subject. What could I do?" Discuss students' responses.

4. Point out one or two subheadings in the section and ask volunteers to read them aloud. Explain that authors sometimes divide sections of text into subsections headed by smaller headings called *subheadings*.

5. Tell students that headings and subheadings can help them see how an author has organized the information in a book or piece of writing. Use the heading and subheadings to write an informal outline of the chapter on the board, such as this one from *Pocket Pets*:

<u>Gerbil</u>
The Origin of Pet Gerbils
A Gerbil's Life
Gerbils as Pets

6. Remind students that they can use headings and subheadings to get an idea of what a section of writing is about (to preview), to find information while they read, and to review material they've already read. Suggest that noticing headings and subheadings will help them better understand and remember what they read.

Status of the Class Follow-Up

As you take the Status of the Class, ask:
- How is the information in this book organized?
- Have you recently read a book that contains headings and subheadings? What was the book about?
- How did the headings help you understand the information given in the book?

If the student is currently reading a book with headings and subheadings, ask:
- What does the main heading of this section tell you?
- What do the subheadings tell you?

Added Practice

- If students are using a textbook or other reference book for research, ask them to keep a list of headings and subheadings from the section or chapter they are reading. Discuss how they can use the notes to remember what they read.
- Give pairs of students a textbook or reference book containing headings. Suggest that partners each list five items of information highlighted by headings or subheadings in the book. Have them exchange the lists and see how long it takes them to locate each item on the list.
- Suggest that students use headings to organize information in their own written reports.

Imagery

Objective To help students focus on imagery when reading

Materials Any book you have recently read to students, such as *Charlotte's Web* by E.B. White (4.4)

Lesson

1. Have students pretend that you are a person who has never visited a school cafeteria before. Tell them that you want to know everything there is to know about their lunchroom. Ask them to describe the setting using details that help you understand what the cafeteria looks, sounds, feels, smells, and tastes like.

2. Choose words from their descriptions that are specific and vivid. Record the words on the board. Help students recognize that a phrase like "stinks of spaghetti sauce combined with floor polish" gives you a much clearer understanding of the cafeteria than simply the word "smells."

3. Tell students that authors carefully choose details that appeal to the five senses to help readers imagine a setting or what is happening in a story. This use of words is called *imagery*. Choose a passage from the book you are reading aloud that demonstrates the use of *imagery*. For instance, you might read this passage from *Charlotte's Web*—the day that Wilbur gets a buttermilk bath:

   > Wilbur stood still and closed his eyes. He could feel buttermilk trickling down his sides. He opened his mouth and some buttermilk ran into it. It was delicious. He felt radiant and happy. When Mrs. Zuckerman got through and rubbed him dry, he was the cleanest, prettiest pig you ever saw.

4. Point out that authors choose words not only to give readers a picture of what is happening, but also to create a feeling. Ask, "Is having a buttermilk bath a pleasant or an unpleasant experience?" (pleasant). "What words does the author use to make you think that?" (*delicious, trickle, cleanest, prettiest*).

5. Read another passage with contrasting imagery and ask, "How do you feel when you hear this passage?" In the following description, E.B. White still talks of food, but uses different imagery:

   > In the hard-packed dirt of the midway, after the glaring lights are out and the people have gone to bed, you will find a veritable treasure of popcorn fragments, frozen custard dribblings, candied apples abandoned by tired children, sugar fluff crystals, salted almonds, popsicles, partially gnawed ice cream cones and wooden sticks of lollypops.

   Ask, "What kind of feeling has the author created in this passage?" (worn-out, used, disgusting). "What words make you think that?" (*dribblings, abandoned, partially gnawed*).

6. Go back to the description of the cafeteria that the students provided. Ask, "Does your description create a feeling about as well as a picture of the cafeteria? Have you used specific words that appeal to the five senses?" Point out their effective uses of imagery.

Status of the Class Follow-Up

As you take the Status of the Class, ask:
- Can you find an example of imagery in the book that you are reading?
- How does that description make you feel?
- What words does the author use to create that feeling?
- Which of the five senses does the author call upon you to use?

Added Practice

- Create a chart on the blackboard with these five headings: *taste, see, smell, hear, touch*. Have the students generate a list of words to go under each heading. For instance, under *taste* might be the words *sour, sweet, tangy, moldy*. Under *hear* might be the words *buzzing, yelling, humming*. As students read independently, have them add sensory words to the classroom chart.
- For a week or two, invite children to find wonderful examples of imagery in the books they are reading and take turns reading them at a specially designated time. You might want to create an "imagery sign-up sheet" to help students keep this goal in mind.
- Ask students to write short, vivid descriptions of a favorite setting (the beach, a movie theater, inside a snow fort), without mentioning what the setting is. Invite classmates to guess the location the sketch describes.

Similes and Metaphors

Objective To help students recognize how writers use comparisons (similes and metaphors) to create images in poetry

Materials "Birches" by Robert Frost (illustrated by Ed Young), or another illustrated poem that contains examples of similes and metaphors

Lesson

1. Display the cover illustration of "Birches" and ask, "What words or phrases would you use to describe this scene?" Record students' responses on the board.

2. Read aloud your chosen poem, displaying the illustrations as you read. Point out that just as artists use drawings and color to illustrate ideas, writers use carefully chosen words to paint pictures or images in the reader's mind. Reread the poem, stopping after a metaphor, such as this one from "Birches":

    Such heaps of broken glass to sweep away

3. Ask students, "Is the poet really talking about broken glass here? What is he comparing to broken glass?" Explain that by comparing the ice on the tree to "heaps of broken glass" the poet is creating a picture in the reader's mind.

4. Continue reading, pausing after a simile. For example:

    . . . trailing their leaves on the ground

    Like girls on hands and knees that throw their hair

    Before them over their heads to dry in the sun.

5. Ask students, "What are the birches being compared to here?" (girls who are drying their hair). Reread the lines, emphasizing the word *like*. Tell students, "The words *like* and *as* often signal comparisons." If you wish, point out that comparisons that use the words *like* or *as* are called *similes*.

6. Ask students to look for ways that writers use comparisons to create images in the books that they are reading. Tell students that being aware of how writers use comparisons to create images in their minds will help them better understand and enjoy the poetry and other materials they read.

Status of the Class Follow-Up

As you take the Status of the Class, ask:
- Have you read any poems recently? What was the poem about?
- Do you remember any pictures that the poem created in your mind? What were they?
- Have you found any comparisons in the book that you are currently reading? What two things is the writer comparing?

Added Practice

- Have students look through collections of poetry to find poems containing comparisons. As students read aloud their chosen poems, have them point out the images being compared and record the phrases on the chart.
- Suggest that groups of students brainstorm lists of comparisons (similes or metaphors) for a common item or animal. For example:

    <u>Cat</u>

    like a dark shadow

    a big bag of bones

    as soft as silk
- Encourage individual students to write their own poems, using comparisons to create images.

Characterization

Objective To help students identify the relationship between a character's actions and his or her motives

Materials Any story or novel you have recently read to students, such as *Stone Fox* by John Reynolds Gardiner (4.0)

Lesson

1. Tell students that in many stories, a character wants to do something very much and that it is this wanting (or *motive*) that causes the character to act in a certain way. Give examples of familiar fictional characters and ask students to tell you what each character wants:
   - Cinderella (to go to the ball)
   - The duckling from "The Ugly Duckling" (to be accepted)
   - Wilbur in *Charlotte's Web* (to stay alive)

2. Tell students that what causes a character to do something is called the character's *motive*. Help students identify the motives of the main character in the story that you are currently reading aloud. For example, ask, "In *Stone Fox*, what does Willy want?" (to earn $500 to pay the taxes on his grandfather's farm).

3. Ask, "What does Willy's desire cause him to do?" Record students' responses on the board. Possible student responses include:

   - He asks friends and neighbors for advice.
   - He goes to the bank to request a loan.
   - He enters a dogsled race.

4. Point out that Willy's actions in the story are closely connected to his desires. Explain that a well-written story includes mainly actions that push the character toward getting what he or she wants. (For instance, Willy does not go on a field trip because that action doesn't relate to his goal of earning enough money to save the farm.)

5. You may want to mention that in some longer works of fiction, the main character changes his mind about what he or she wants and therefore the actions change, too. For instance, in the beginning of *The Wizard of Oz*, Dorothy wants to run away from home; this motivates one course of action (leaving home and getting caught in the tornado). Once Dorothy arrives in Oz, however, she wants nothing more than to return home, which causes another course of action.

6. Tell students that thinking about the main character's motives will help them better understand the character's actions and predict what his or her future actions might be.

Status of the Class Follow-Up

As you take the Status of the Class, ask:
- What does the main character in your story want?
- What action does your main character take to get what he or she wants?
- Does the author put obstacles in the path of your main character? Why do you think the author does that?

Added Practice

- Have students list the motives of the main characters in books they are reading. Record their responses on the chalkboard. How many common motives are there? Guide students to understand that many characters want the same things (to find a home, to find a friend, to be accepted), but they go about getting what they want in different ways.
- Tell students that a story would be pretty dull if the character set out to get what he or she wanted and then got it immediately. Point out that authors place obstacles in the path of the character to make the story more exciting or suspenseful and to show you more about the type of person a character is. Mention a character from a book you have recently read to the class. Have the students list the roadblocks the author put in the character's path. Then list the actions the character took to get around each roadblock.

Plot: Conflict and Resolution

Objective To introduce the plot pattern of conflict leading to resolution

Materials Any story or novel that you have read recently that has a clear problem and solution in the plot, such as *Holes* by Louis Sachar (4.6)

Lesson

1. Help students recall the plot of the book you've chosen. Remind them that the *plot* is what happens in the story and that plots are often organized around a problem and a solution. For example, in the story of *Holes*, Stanley Yelnats is falsely accused of stealing sneakers and is forced to spend his days digging holes at a detention camp.

2. Create a story diagram on the board that demonstrates rising action. Write the problem at the base of the diagonal line.

Stanley is sent to camp.

3. Ask, "How did you feel when Stanley was sent to camp and had to endure a number of trials?" (angry, nervous, anxious for Stanley). Tell students that authors create problems or *conflict* to build suspense. It is conflict that keeps the reader turning the pages and wondering how it will turn out in the end.

4. Mention to students that in most cases, the main character attempts to solve his or her own problem. Ask, "What did Stanley Yelnats do to solve his problem?" Possible answers might be:
   - He searched for something interesting.
   - He ran off to find Zero.
   - He helped Zero get back to camp.
   - He dug again in the hole where he had found something.

   Write the character's attempts along the diagonal line of your story diagram.

5. Tell students that the *resolution* of the story is the point at which the problem has been solved. Ask, "What point was the resolution of this story?" (When the lawyer rescues Stanley and Zero from the hole—and from Camp Greenwood.) Write the resolution at the top point of your diagram.

6. Point out that authors often create many questions that keep the reader curious enough to read on after the resolution of the main conflict, and that those questions are usually answered, or "wrapped up," after the resolution. Ask students to tell you what questions they had while listening to the Read To book. Ask, "Were all of your questions answered in the end?"
7. Ask students to identify the conflict in the books they are reading, and predict what the resolution might be.

Status of the Class Follow-Up

As you take the Status of the Class, ask:
- Are you reading fiction? If so, what is the conflict in your story, or this part of your story? (Most children's stories follow the conflict/resolution pattern. However, stories can be episodic in which case each chapter or group of chapters may have a small conflict of its own.)
- What was the last story or novel that you read? What was the conflict in that story? What was the resolution?
- Were you able to predict the resolution?

Added Practice

- Raise this question: "Where does a good story start?" Have children use their favorite literature to investigate this question. They are likely to find that good stories start at the onset or right in the middle of conflict (and not three days before). You may even find examples of stories that begin in the middle of crisis and then use flashbacks to fill in the reader on background information.
- As students read independently, have them record their predictions of how a story will end. Later, discuss the accuracy of their predictions. Then ask, "What do you know about resolutions that help you to make predictions?" (The main problem is solved, and outstanding questions or loose ends are wrapped up.)
- Invite students to write a different ending, or resolution, to a favorite story.

Setting

Objective To help students identify the time and place in which events in a selection occur and recognize how setting affects plot

Materials Any story with an integral setting, such as *My Brother Sam Is Dead* by James Lincoln Collier and Christopher Collier (4.9)

Lesson

1. Read aloud the first chapter of *My Brother Sam Is Dead* or an appropriate section of your current Read To book. As you read, record students' answers to the following questions. For example:
   - Where does most of this story take place? (mostly Connecticut, in the American colonies).
   - When does this story take place? (during the American Revolution).

2. Remind students that the time and place in which the events of a story take place are called the *setting*. Draw the following chart on the board.

3. Ask students to find details from the story that tell about where and when the story takes place. Record the information in the chart. For example:

TIME	PLACE
Sam talks about the Patriots beating the British at Lexington and Concord.	"There's a lot more Tories in this part of Connecticut than in the rest of the colonies."

4. Tell students that the setting of a book is important because it often affects the actions of the characters and the events, or *plot*, of the story. Ask, "Could the events in this story be the same if it were set in a different time or place? Could the same events take place today? How might Sam's actions be different if the story were set in England rather than the American colonies?"

5. Review the details listed in the chart and discuss how each one affects the action of the plot. For example, "A lot of the action in *My Brother Sam Is Dead* takes place in Tim's house. Why is it important that his house is also a tavern and a store?" (Strangers and local people stopping in at the tavern and store share gossip, so Tim and his family are often among the first to hear any news of the war and other events.) Ask students to look for details about setting in their books and to think about how the setting affects what happens in the story.

Status of the Class Follow-Up

As you take the Status of the Class, ask:
- Where and when does this story take place?
- What details from the story tell you about the setting?
- Could this story have taken place at a different place or time? Why or why not?
- Does the setting of your book change at any time? How?

Added Practice

- Suggest that students draw maps or illustrations of settings from their books. Mount the illustrations on heavy paper and cut them into pieces to make jigsaw puzzles. Encourage students to exchange puzzles and predict the stories' settings as they work one another's puzzles.
- Invite students to use pictures from magazines to make a collage representing the setting of their book.
- Create a class chart listing books with similar settings. For example, books set during the Revolutionary War might include *Sarah Bishop*, *The Fighting Ground*, and *Why Don't You Get a Horse, Sam Adams*?

Theme

Objective To help students infer and identify the central idea or theme of a story

Materials *Pegasus, the Flying Horse* by Jane Yolen (4.3) or another fiction book that can be read in one sitting

Lesson

1. Explain that the *theme* of a story is the "big idea" or meaning behind the story. Quickly review the main events of a popular "good versus evil" action movie or television show, such as *Star Wars*. Then write on the board:

   Good is more powerful than evil.

2. Explain that the theme of a story is not just what happens in the story, but rather what the author's point is in telling the story—what the story is all about. Emphasize the following points:
   - A theme is usually a statement about life or how people should act.
   - An author may not state a theme directly. Sometimes the author implies the theme through the characters' actions or words.
   - A story may have more than one theme.

3. Tell students that you are going to read them a story. Ask them to try to figure out the theme of the story as you read it.

4. Read the story, but not the author's note at the beginning. Ask, "What is the theme of this story?" List students' responses on the board. Students' suggestions might include:

   - **Don't fly too high.**
   - **Finding a horse.**
   - **People who are too proud will be punished in the end.**

5. Discuss students' suggestions by asking clarifying questions such as, "Is this story really just about flying? What point do you think the author wants to make about people in general?" Remind students that no two readers are likely to state a theme in exactly the same way. You may wish to read the author's note to help students identify the theme.

6. After the class has agreed on a theme, draw the following diagram on the board. Write the theme statement in the heart. Ask, "What words or actions from the book show this theme?" Record students' responses in the circle sections surrounding the heart.

7. Tell students that figuring out a book's theme will help them better understand what they read.

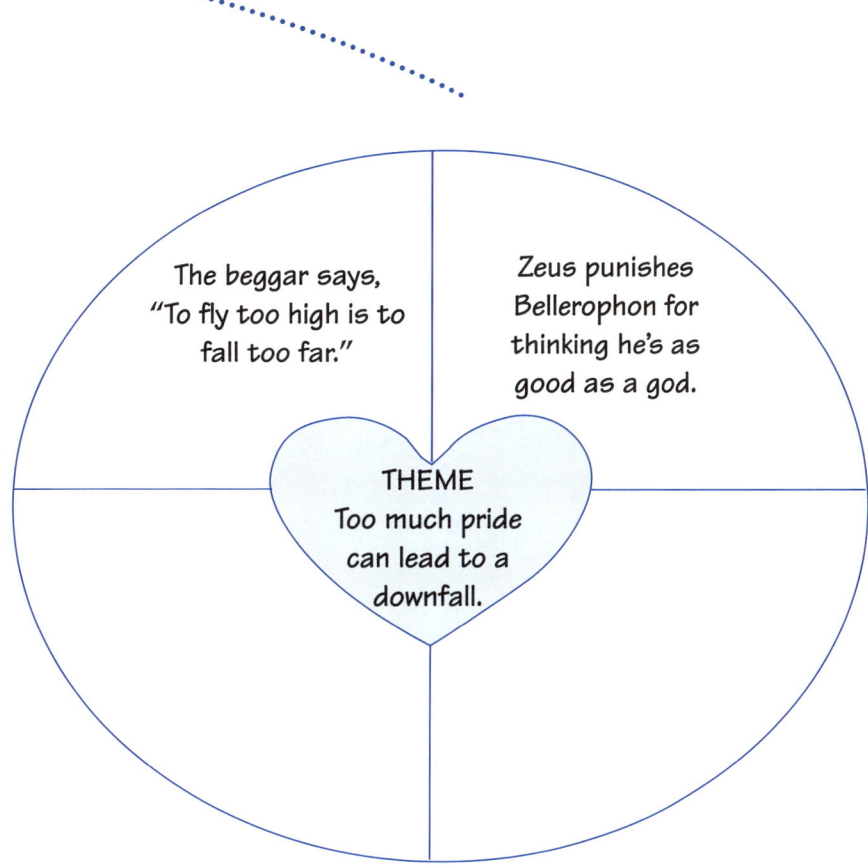

Status of the Class Follow-Up

As you take the Status of the Class, ask:
- What is the main theme of your book?
- Which words or actions show that theme?
- Are there other themes in your book? What are they?

Added Practice

- Encourage students to complete diagrams like the one above listing the theme of a fiction book they are currently reading and details that support the theme.
- As you discuss books in class, keep a list of common themes. Encourage students to refer to the list and note which themes recur frequently.
- Suggest that groups of students write and act out a skit expressing the theme of a book they have recently read.

Tone

Objective To help students recognize the tone of a piece of writing and explain how writers use word choice and other elements of style to create tone

Materials Copies of the poems "Crocodile" (Anonymous) and "The Crocodile" by Michael Flanders (page 59) for each student

Lesson

1. Have a student knock on the door of the classroom. Answer in a cheerful voice, "Come in!" Ask a different student to knock again. This time answer "Come in!" in an angry voice. Ask a third student to knock again, and answer in a sad or resigned voice.

2. Ask students, "Did my words change each time someone knocked on the door? What changed?" Explain that a speaker's tone of voice can tell a lot about how the person feels about what is happening. Ask, "What was my tone of voice the first time someone knocked? The second time? The last time?"

3. Tell students that writers, like speakers, show how they feel about a subject through the *tone* of their writing. Explain that since a reader usually can't hear an author's tone of voice, the writer must rely on the words themselves to express his or her attitude toward the subject.

4. Tell students that you are going to read aloud two poems about crocodiles. Say, "As I read each poem, think about the writer's attitude toward the crocodile. Is it serious or lighthearted, respectful or scornful, sorrowful or rejoicing?"

5. Read aloud the first poem ("Crocodile"). Ask, "What words or phrases does the writer use to describe how the crocodile looks and acts?" Record the words or phrases on the board. Lead students to conclude that the tone of the poem is serious and respectful by asking questions such as, "What do these words and phrases tell you about the author's attitude toward the crocodile? Are they serious or silly? Do they seem respectful, or do they make fun of the subject?"

6. Follow the same procedure with "The Crocodile" by Michael Flanders. Then ask, "Are the tones of these poems the same or different? Which poem do you like better? Why?" Explain that thinking about the tone, or how a writer views his or her subject, will help students better understand what they read.

Status of the Class Follow-Up

As you take the Status of the Class, ask:
- What is the tone of this part of your book? Is it serious or humorous?
- Can you read me a passage that shows that tone?
- What specific words does the author use to express that tone?

Added Practice

- Suggest that students create color illustrations that express the tone of each of the poems.
- Have students write two paragraphs—one serious and the other light-hearted or humorous—about the same subject.
- Remind students that the tone of a story can change as the story moves along. Have them chart the changes of tone that occur in their books as they read.

Crocodile

Ancient reptile
Silent log in still green waters
Danger in disguise.

—*Anonymous*

The Crocodile

This is a Crocodile, my boy…
Or is it an Alligator?…
I've an excellent book that you'll enjoy
We can refer to later;

The Alligator…no, Crocodile
Is a purplish color beneath.
Give it a tickle to make it smile
And let's count the number of teeth,

For the Croc (I think) has a row too few
Though the Gator can't wink its eye…

Ah!
   Now I can tell you which of the two
You have just been eaten by.

—*Michael Flanders*

Biography and Autobiography

Objective To help students identify biography and autobiography, recognizing that they are types of nonfiction

Materials Any biography and autobiography that you have recently read (or could read briefly) such as *Rosa Parks* by Eloise Greenfield (4.0) and *26 Fairmount Avenue* by Tomie DePaola (4.4)

Lesson

1. Ask students to think for a moment: "What if someone chose to write your life story? What would he or she say about you? What events from your life might be told?" Give students a few moments to reflect and invite volunteers to share their ideas.

2. Tell students that a factual story of someone else's life is called a *biography*. Because biographies tell about real people, places, and events, they are nonfiction.

3. Hold up the biography you have chosen. Ask, "What do you know about this person?" Record student responses on the chalkboard. Then ask, "Why do you think the author chose to write about this person?" Possible responses for Rosa Parks might be:

   - Rosa was brave.
   - Her life tells us about a time in history.
   - Her actions helped change history.

   Guide students to understand that we read biographies to learn about the past, to think about and sometimes be inspired by other people, and to ask ourselves, "What would I do if I were in the same situation?"

4. Choose one item from the list and ask, "Where do you think the author got this information?" Help students understand that authors get information from various sources, including historical records, journals, and letters. If a subject is still living, the author might interview him or her.

5. Now draw attention to the autobiography you have chosen. Read a selection to demonstrate the difference in point of view (first person versus third person). For instance, you might read the opening sentences from *26 Fairmount Avenue*:

   > I didn't always live in the house at 26 Fairmount Avenue. We moved there when I was five years old. I know that because in 1938, when I was still four, a big hurricane hit Meriden, Connecticut, where we lived.

   Tell students that a story about a person's life written by that person is called an *autobiography*.

6. Ask students, "Why might someone write the story of his or her own life?" Possible answers might include:
   - The author wants to share personal stories.
   - The author knows the details best.
   - The author might disagree with the way another person would write the story.
7. Point out that biographies and autobiographies need not cover a person's entire life—they might present only one time in the person's life. For example, Eloise Greenfield chose to focus on the time that Rosa Parks refused to go to the back of the bus and Tomie DePaola chose to write about the year that he moved into his new home.
8. Ask, "What if someone else wrote Tomie DePaola's story? How might it be different? Do you think someone else would think that moving into a new house was very important?"
9. Discuss the way in which a biography and an autobiography about the same person might differ. Help students understand that although a biographer and autobiographer present information, they each have to choose which information gets told and decide what the information means.

Status of the Class Follow-Up

As you take the Status of the Class, ask:
- Have you read a biography or an autobiography lately? Who was it about?
- What was one thing you learned from the biography or autobiography?
- If you were going to choose a biography or autobiography to read next, what person would you enjoy reading about? Why?

Added Practice

- Have students make a two-column chart. In the first column, students can record interesting information they learn while reading a biography. In the second column, encourage students to speculate where the author may have found this information. Help students understand that although some information may be found in reference books such as encyclopedias, biographers prefer to find as many actual (primary) documents as they can. For instance, if a biographer were telling Tomie DePaola's story, he might look at a receipt for the sale of land at 26 Fairmount Avenue.
- Suggest that students read a biography and an autobiography of the same person. (Both biographies and autobiographies have been written about Helen Keller, Roald Dahl, and Magic Johnson for starters.) Ask students to consider the following questions while reading:
  – Which book gave you more information about the person?
  – Which book made you feel as if you knew the person better? Why?
  – Which type of life story did you prefer? Why?

Historical Fiction

Objective To help students compare historical fiction to contemporary realistic fiction

Materials Two books—one contemporary realistic fiction, one historical fiction—that deal with similar themes such as *A Year With Butch and Spike* by Gail Gauthier (4.7) and *Number the Stars* by Lois Lowry (4.5)

Lesson
1. Show students the books you have chosen and remind them of themes that the books have in common. Using the books mentioned above, you might say: "In both of these books, the main character helps and defends a friend who is being mistreated. Yet the books have some important differences as well."

2. Remind students that a setting of a story is the place and time in which the story took place. Hold up the contemporary realistic fiction book you have chosen. Ask students, "What is the setting of this story?" (The Theodore Ervin Elementary School in any town, during the present time.) Ask, "Could this story take place in recent times? How do you know?" Possible answers might be:
   - The modern language and expressions the kids use
   - The mention of topics such as cloning and zines
   - The clothing, food, and objects described in the book

3. Hold up the historical fiction book you have selected and ask: "What is the setting of this book?" (Copenhagen, Denmark, in 1943). Tell students that this story is historical fiction—fiction that takes place in the past—and that historical fiction is a combination of fiction and fact about a certain place at a certain time. Ask, "What details helped you to know and understand the setting of this story?" Possible answers might include:
   - The unusual spelling of Danish names
   - The presence of German soldiers in Copenhagen

4. Point out that contemporary or modern realistic fiction can often take place in any town, now or during any years in recent history, but historical fiction is always written about a specific place during a specific time. (You might point out that authors of contemporary realistic fiction often make up the names of their towns.) Tell students that sometimes the author includes notes in the back of historical fiction that help the reader to determine which parts of the book were factual and which parts were fiction. For instance, in her afterword, Lois Lowry explains which events in the book actually did happen in Denmark in the 1940s.

5. Tell that it is important to figure the time and place in which a story occurs and to think about what effect time and place has on what takes place in the story.

Status of the Class Follow-Up

As you take the Status of the Class, ask:
- Are you reading a fiction book? Is it historical fiction? Why or why not?
- Have you read any historical fiction lately? How did you know that it was historical?
- What was the setting of your story? Could the events in the story have happened at another place and time?
- Did you learn anything new from the story?

Added Practice

- Invite students to read other historical fiction selections that are written about the same time period as your Read To or their independent selection. How are the books similar? How do they differ?
- Make a class time line and have students write the titles of historical fiction they have read in appropriate places along the line.
- Have students choose two books, one contemporary and one historical, that deal with the same theme. Then ask them to compare and contrast the settings of the books using a Venn diagram.

Context Clues

Objective To help students use the context of one or more paragraphs to infer the meaning of new words

Materials Any story you are currently reading to students, such as *The Family Under the Bridge* by Natalie Savage Carlson (4.7)

Lesson

1. From your current Read To book, read a paragraph or several short paragraphs that contain an unfamiliar word. Search for text that does not give the explicit meaning of the word, but provides clues in the surrounding text, such as the following example from *The Family Under the Bridge*:

   > They stopped their play as Armand went by. "Look at that funny old tramp!" one cried to his playmates.
   >
   > Armand looked around because he wanted to see the funny old tramp too. It must be that droll Louis with his tall black hat and baggy pants. Then he realized that he was the funny old tramp.
   >
   > "Keep a civil tongue in your head, starling" he ordered. He fingered the holly in his lapel. "If you don't, I'll tell my friend Father Christmas about your rude manners. Then you'll get nothing but a bunch of sticks like these on my buggy."

2. Ask, "If you see an unfamiliar word like *civil* when you're reading, what are some of the ways that you can figure out the word?" Reread the selection and ask, "What other words in that sentence can help you figure out the word *civil*?"

3. Explain to students that good readers have strategies for using the other words and sentences, or *context clues*, to figure out unfamiliar words. Discuss strategies for figuring out unfamiliar words, such as:

   - Look for *clues*, such as antonyms, synonyms, and examples:
     - "Keep a civil tongue in your head, starling" he ordered. He fingered the holly in his lapel. "If you don't, I'll tell my friend Father Christmas about your rude manners." (antonym)
     - The gypsy boys, followed by Paul, disappeared into the tents. Most of the men were gone, but the few remaining ones vanished as quickly as the boys. (synonym)
     - It must be that droll Louis with his tall black hat and baggy pants. (example)

   - Use *common sense*. What else is happening in the story? Who says the word, to whom, and why?

     "No need, madame," he said as haughtily as he had spoken to the floorwalker. "I'll leave myself and save you the trouble. I know when I'm not welcome."

Ask yourself, how did Armand talk to the floorwalker? What tone would he use to say, "I know when I'm not welcome?"

4. Ask students to look in their books for two unfamiliar words and to be prepared to tell how they used the context to figure out each word's meaning.

Status of the Class Follow-Up

As you take the Status of the Class, ask:
- Have you run into any unfamiliar words in your book?
- Did you use the context to help you figure out the meaning of the word? What strategies did you use?
- What could you do if there were no clues in the surrounding paragraphs to help you figure out the meaning of the word? (Look in the dictionary. Rely on common sense.)

Added Practice
- Suggest that students make a three-column chart (like the one below) to use while they are reading. In the first column they list unfamiliar words. In the second column, they write down their predictions of what the words mean based on context clues. The third column is a place to record the dictionary definition after the student has finished reading. How close did the student predictions come to the dictionary definition?

New word	Prediction	Dictionary definition

- Have each student find an unfamiliar word in the dictionary and use it in a paragraph that contains either a synonym or antonym of that word. Encourage students to read their sentences aloud and ask others to predict the meaning of the unknown word. Which word gave the context clue?

Homonyms

Objective To help students to recognize homonyms and use context clues to determine their meanings

Materials Any story you have recently read such as *Snowdrops for Cousin Ruth* by Susan Katz (4.5)

Lesson

1. Choose several passages from your story that contain a homonym (word with multiple meanings). Then write the homonyms on the chalkboard. For example, you might write these words from *Snowdrops for Cousin Ruth*: *top*, *right*, *spot*.

2. Ask students, "What is the meaning of these words?" Record their responses under each word. Encourage students to think of multiple meanings. Possible responses:

top	right	spot
the highest part	correct	stain
a cover for something	the opposite of <u>left</u>	the name of a dog
	exactly	place

3. Tell students that words that have more than one meaning are called *homonyms* and that they can often determine the intended meaning by reading the words that come before and after.

4. Read the passages that contain the words. Ask students to tell you each word's meaning. For example:
   - She flung her hands to one side, then the other, and spun in a circle like a pink-and-blue *top*. (a spinning toy)
   - She was sitting *right* up front with the driver. (in the exact location)
   - Even Clyde would uncurl from his favorite *spot* on the empty bottom shelf of the cart where Momma kept the microwave. (place)
   - Put a check next to the correct meaning on your lists, or add a new definition if necessary.

5. Write some homographs on the chalkboard, such as:

   bow
   desert
   present

Ask students to tell you the meaning of each word. They will no doubt discover that the meanings depend on how each word is pronounced. Guide students to understand that the meaning of a *homograph*—a word that has the same spelling, but more than one pronunciation and meaning—can also be determined by reading the words that come before and after.

6. Tell students, "If you come to a word you know that doesn't make sense in the sentence, think about whether it might be a word that has more than one meaning. Then look for clues in the sentences around it that will help you figure out its meaning."

7. Ask students to look for homonyms and homographs as they read their books. You might also wish to pause briefly to point out homonyms as you read during Read To time.

Status of the Class Follow-Up

As you take the Status of the Class, ask:
- Have you found any homonyms or homographs in your book?
- Which meaning of the word makes sense in this sentence? What other words in the sentence helped you figure out the homonym's meaning?
- What could you do if there were no clues in the sentence to help you figure out the meaning of the homonym? (Look the word up in a dictionary. Continue reading and come back to the word later.)

Added Practice

- Create a master homonym list. Divide a large sheet of butcher paper into alphabetical sections. Encourage students to record on the list any homonyms they come across in books. You may even wish to set up a friendly competition between groups of students or classes to see whose list is longest at the end of a certain amount of time.
- Play Multiple Meanings. Choose a homonym such as the word *level*. Participants take turns using the word in a sentence without repeating the same meaning. For instance:

  – The car is parked on the first level.

  – Hand me the level so I can see if the floor is flat.

  – The card house is built on a level surface.

  The player who comes up with the last sentence gets to pick the next homonym.

Synonyms and Antonyms

Objective To help students use synonyms and antonyms to figure out words in context

Materials *The Wheel on the School* by Meindert DeJong (4.7) or another Read To book containing examples of synonyms or antonyms in context

Lesson

1. Remind students that a *synonym* is a word that means the same or nearly the same as another word. Draw the following word web for *boat* on the board. Ask students to help you complete the web by suggesting synonyms for the word *boat*.

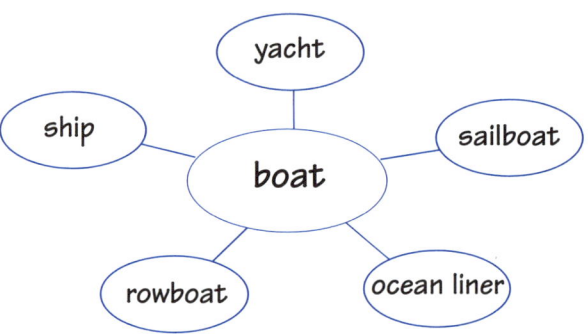

2. Write on the board and read aloud a passage, preferably from your current Read To book, that contains an unfamiliar word and its synonym, for example, this passage from *The Wheel on the School*:

   This time the <u>dinghy</u> had to be left behind. The sea was too roiled to risk hoisting it on board the boat of Jella's father to serve as a lifeboat for the little fishing fleet.

3. Ask, "What does the word *dinghy* mean? Which other words in these sentences helped you figure out the meaning of *dinghy*?" (lifeboat)

4. Explain to students that one way to figure out the meaning of unfamiliar words is to look for clues, such as synonyms, that help them understand the word's meaning.

5. Next, ask students what a word's *opposite* is called (an antonym). Draw another word web for the word *wild* and have students supply antonyms to complete the web (tame, calm, mild, controllable).

6. Write on the board and read aloud a passage containing an unfamiliar word and its antonym, such as this one from *A Wheel on the School*. Ask students which words in the passage help them figure out the meaning of *meek*.

   "Hey, hold their necks!" Janus suddenly warned. "They're still wild, even if they are pretty <u>meek</u> now."

7. Tell students that antonyms, too, can serve as clues that will help them figure out the meanings of unfamiliar words.
8. Ask students to look in their books for synonyms and antonyms that help them figure out the meanings of unfamiliar words.

Status of the Class Follow-Up

As you take the Status of the Class, ask:
- Have you run into any synonyms or antonyms in your book?
- Did knowing that the words were synonyms or antonyms help you figure out the meaning of the sentences?
- What other clues can you use if you don't know the meaning of a word?

Added Practice

- Have students keep lists of synonyms and antonyms that they run across in their reading. You may wish to record students' findings on a giant class chart of synonyms and antonyms.
- Suggest that pairs of students write out paragraphs from books they are currently reading. Have students exchange papers and then rewrite each others' paragraphs, replacing four or five key words with their antonyms. Encourage students to read aloud the new paragraphs and discuss the changes in meaning.

Consonant Variants

Objective To help students decode words containing consonant variants and silent letters

Materials Any Read To book with words that contain consonant variants (tou**gh**, techni**que**) or silent letters (**gn**aw) such as *Poppy* by Avi (4.5)

Lesson

1. Write phrases that contain the phonics element(s) you are teaching on the board. To teach *gh*, for example, you might write the following phrases from *Poppy*:

   . . . if there was not <u>enough</u> food . . .
   Spitting and <u>coughing</u> . . .
   . . . she could make a <u>rough</u> determination . . .

2. Ask, "Do you see a word in each phrase that has the same spelling pattern as others?" (enough, cough, rough). Point out that sometimes the letters *gh* represent the same sound as the letter *f* in *fish*.

3. Now ask, "Can you think of other words that follow this letter and sound pattern?" (tough, laugh, trough). Write the words students provide on the board. Circle the *gh* in each word. If students offer words that do not follow the spelling pattern, acknowledge their ability to hear the correct sounds, but do not add the words to the list.

4. If the consonant variant you are teaching also represents other phonemic sounds, you may choose to teach those sounds simultaneously. For example, write a sentence or phrase with the additional sound such as this sentence from *Poppy*:

   Suddenly a ghastly realization came over her.

   Circle the word *ghastly*. Tell students that sometimes the *h* is silent when placed next to *g*. Ask, "Can you think of other words that have *gh* in which the *h* is silent?" (*ghost, ghetto*). Students may come up with other words in which both the *g* and the *h* are silent (*though, through*). If so, acknowledge these spellings as well.

5. Encourage students to look for words that use the targeted spelling pattern as they read. You might suggest that they write down the word and the page number on a slip of paper, so they can point the spelling out at a later time.

Status of the Class Follow-Up

As you take the Status of the Class, ask:
- Did you find any words with *gh*? What sound did the letter combination make?
- How does knowing about this letter combination help you to read the word?

Added Practice
- Invite students to create crossword puzzles. Answers should contain the consonant variant or silent letters you introduced.
- Have students look for words that contain the targeted spelling pattern in newspapers and magazines. They can cut the words out and paste them on a word collage.
- Encourage students to look for words that have different consonant variants. Build new power lessons around the digraphs and variants that students discover, such as:
    - *ch:* cheese, each, chaos
    - *kn:* knowledge, unknown
    - *ph:* phantom, newphew
    - *wr:* wreath, rewrite
    - *hard and soft c:* ceiling, decent, calculate, second
    - *hard and soft g:* gentle, vegetable, garden, wagon, garage

Prefixes That Mean "Not"

Objective   To help students figure out unfamiliar words by recognizing prefixes

Materials   A shoe with shoelaces untied

Lesson

1. Hold up the untied shoe and ask, "What can I do with these shoelaces?" As students answer, tie the laces and write the word *tie* on the board.

2. Remind students that a root word is a word to which other word parts can be added to make new words. Point to the word *tie* and say, "*Tie* can be a root word."

3. Ask, "Suppose I want to put this shoe on. Now what must I do?" Untie the laces and write *untie* on the board. Circle the prefix *un-*. Explain that *un-* is a prefix—a word part added to the beginning of a root word to make a new word. Ask, "If *un-* means 'not,' then what does the word *untie* mean?"

tie

(un)tie

4. Ask students to suggest other words that begin with the prefix *un-*. Record students' suggestions on the board.

5. Tell students that there are other prefixes that also mean "not." Draw the following diagram on the board. Write the following prefixes in the outside boxes: *de-, dis-, ir-, il-, im-, in-, non-, un-*. Ask students to help you think of words that contain each prefix. List the words in the appropriate squares.

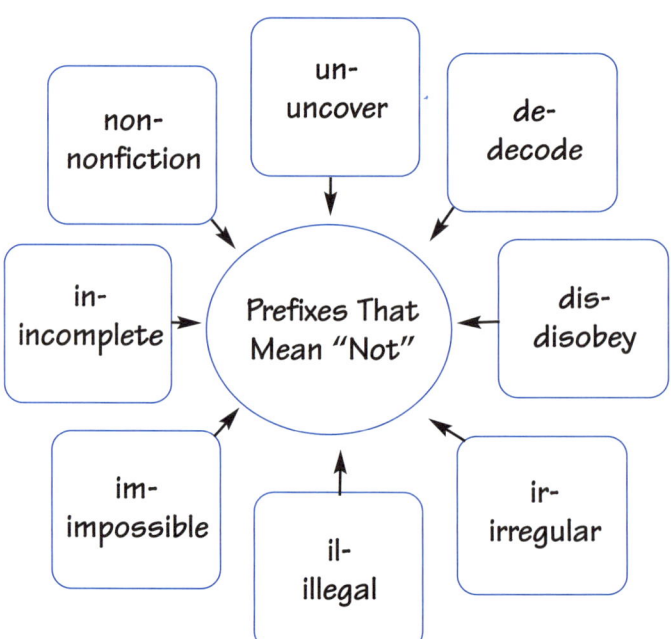

6. Ask students to see if they can find two words that contain prefixes that mean "not" in their books. Tell them that knowing how to break words into prefixes and root words will help them figure out the meaning of unfamiliar words.

Status of the Class Follow-Up

If a student stumbles over a word with a prefix while reading, show her how to frame the root word with her fingers and read the root word first. As you take the Status of the Class, ask:

- Have you found any words that contain prefixes that mean "not"?
- What is the meaning of the root word?
- How does knowing the meaning of the root word and the prefix help you figure out the word's meaning?

Added Practice

- Make copies of the diagram shown on page 72 and hand them out to students. Encourage students to add to the diagram words with negative prefixes that they run across in their reading.
- Encourage pairs of students to challenge each other with "positive/negative" sentences. Have each partner write a sentence in which one word's meaning could be changed by adding a prefix that means *not*. For example:

    – Your handwriting is possible to read.

    – Your handwriting is *impossible* to read.

    Have partners exchange papers, add a prefix to the appropriate word, read aloud the new sentence, and discuss the change in the sentence's meaning.

Suffixes

Objective To help students figure out unfamiliar words by recognizing suffixes

Materials One white and one brightly colored sheet of construction paper

Lesson

1. Write the word *color* in large letters on each sheet of construction paper. Hold up the bright sheet and present the following riddle, "I'm thinking of a word that has the word *color* in it and describes this sheet of paper. What is the word?" Write the suffix *-ful* after the word *color* and have a volunteer read the word aloud.

2. Follow the same procedure, using the white sheet. Write the suffix *-less* after the word *color* and have a student read the word aloud.

3. Explain that a root word is a word to which other word parts can be added to make new words. Point to the word *color* on both sheets and say, "*Color* is a root word."

4. Circle the suffixes *-ful* and *-less*. Explain that word parts added to the end of a root word to make a new word are called *suffixes*. Ask, "If *-ful* means 'full of,' then what does the word *colorful* mean?" Repeat the procedure for *colorless*, asking, "If *-less* means 'without,' what does *colorless* mean?"

5. Write the following suffixes and their meanings on the board. Ask students to look through their books for words that contain the suffixes listed in the chart below. As you write each example on the board, help students identify the root word and suffix. Then have students use the meanings of the root word and suffix to figure out the meaning of the larger word.

SUFFIX	EXAMPLE	MEANING
-ful	hopeful restful	full of
-less	fearless useless	without
-able	enjoyable breakable	can be
-ness	gladness darkness	the state of being
-ment	payment punishment	the act of
-ance	annoyance acceptance	the state of being

Status of the Class Follow-Up

If a student stumbles over a word with a suffix while reading, show him how to frame the root word with his fingers and read the root word first. As you take the Status of the Class, ask:

- Have you found any words that contain suffixes?
- What is the meaning of the root word? What is the meaning of the suffix?
- How does breaking the word into the root word and the suffix help you pronounce the word and figure out its meaning?

Added Practice

- Encourage pairs or groups of students to make up "suffix equations" such as the following. Have students exchange papers and "solve" each others' problems by giving the missing word part and the completed word.
  - use + ___ = without use
  - ___ + ment = the state of being enjoyed
- Create a class suffix chart similar to the one shown on page 74. Encourage students to add to the chart suffixes that they come across in their reading. Help them complete the chart by filling in the suffixes' meanings and example words.

Syllabication

Objective   To help students decode words by dividing them into syllables

Materials   Any fiction or nonfiction book you are currently reading to students, such as *Belle Prater's Boy* by Ruth White (4.4); list of syllabication rules (page 93)

Lesson

1. Remind students that knowing how to divide words into syllables can help them figure out unknown words. Point out that a syllable is a word part that contains one vowel sound. Say a variety of one-, two-, and three-syllable words, emphasizing the vowels sounds, and ask students how many syllables they hear in each word.

2. Remind students that there are rules that can help them divide words into syllables. On the chalkboard, list two or three VCCV words from your current Read To book, such as these, which appear in *Belle Prater's Boy*:

   critter   perfume   window

3. Draw lines between the syllables in the words on the board. Remind students that when two consonants come between two vowels, the word is usually divided between the two consonants: (crit | ter).

4. Next, write three or four two-syllable words with the VCV pattern, such as these from *Belle Prater's Boy*:

   panic   rotate
   tragic   paper

5. Tell students, "When one consonant comes between two vowels, you may have to try dividing the word in two different ways. First, try dividing the word before the consonant and giving the vowel a long vowel sound: (ro | tate). If that doesn't work, divide the word after the consonant and give the vowel a short sound: (pan | ic). Have volunteers divide and pronounce the words on the board.

6. Follow the same procedure, using words that end with *le* (puzzle, ladle). Tell students, "When a word ends with a consonant and *le*, divide the word before the consonant."

7. Hand out the list of syllabication rules. Ask students to look in their books to find words that follow each rule. Tell students that they can refer to the list whenever they have difficulty figuring out unfamiliar words.

Status of the Class Follow-Up

As you take the Status of the Class, point out a word that follows one of the syllabication rules on the list on page 93. Ask:
- How would you divide this word into syllables?
- Can you read the first syllable? How about the second syllable?
- Now put the syllables together again. Can you read the whole word?
- Have you found any other words that follow one of the syllabication rules on your list?

Added Practice
- Suggest that students keep a running list of words that follow the syllabication rules they have studied. As they read, have them list their words in the sections next to the appropriate rule on the list on page 93.
- Encourage pairs of students to challenge each other by writing lists of three- and four-syllable words from their independent reading. Have students exchange lists and divide words from one anothers' lists into syllables.

Dictionary Skills

Objective To teach students how to use the pronunciation respelling and the pronunciation key in a dictionary

Materials Any book you are currently reading to students, such as *101 Ways to Bug Your Parents* by Lee Wardlaw (3.9); a student dictionary; reproducible sheet of dictionary entries (optional)

Lesson

1. On the board, write a sentence that contains an unfamiliar word and few context clues, for example, you might use this sentence from *101 Ways to Bug Your Parents*:

   "Time is but a <u>trifle</u>," Hiccup said.

2. Ask, "What do you do, if while reading, you come to a word you don't know?" Discuss students' suggestions. Conclude the discussion by saying, "Today we're going to talk about how to figure out the meaning and the *pronunciation* of a word by looking it up in the dictionary." Tell students that the pronunciation is how we say the word.

3. Turn to the page in a student dictionary that has the word *trifle*. Write the dictionary entry on the board or pass out a reproducible sheet.

   trifle \'trī-fəl\ – noun, trifles 1. Something that is unimportant. 2. Something that is smaller in amount.
   verb, 1. To treat something or someone in a careless manner.

4. Show students the respelling. Explain that dictionaries use a code—or respelling—set off by diagonal lines to help readers pronounce words. The respelling shows how words are broken into syllables and uses symbols to show sounds. It also includes accent marks, which tell you which syllable gets the most stress or force when you say a word.

5. Tell students that dictionaries have a key to the respelling on every page. Point to the *pronunciation key* in the dictionary or on the reproducible pages. Show students how to use the key to determine the pronunciation of *trifle*. In doing so, mention the following:
   - For most consonants, use the sound you hear for the letter. Letters that have more than one sound may be represented by a different letter (such as *k* for the hard *c* sound) or a combination of letters (*zh* for the *s* in *vision*).
   - Vowels usually have special symbols. Look in the pronunciation key to see how to pronounce each symbol.
   - If a word has two or more accent marks, place more stress on the syllable with the darker mark and a lighter stress on the syllable with a lighter mark.

6. Have students determine the pronunciation of the word you have chosen and determine which of the dictionary meanings fits the sentence context.
7. Tell students that knowing how to use the dictionary will help them figure out new words when they come across them in their books.

Status of the Class Follow-Up

As you take the Status of the Class, ask:
- Have you come across any words that you don't know the meaning of or that you're not sure how to pronounce?
- Can you show me how to look this word up in the dictionary?
- How do you pronounce the word?

Added Practice

- Give students copies of a pronunciation key and have them write messages to each other in respellings.
- Provide students with a list of homographs (words that are spelled the same but have different pronunciation and meanings such as *bow, wind, wound*). Have students look up the words, determine their pronunciation and meanings, and write sentences to demonstrate their understanding. Ask students to read the sentences aloud to hear differences in pronunciation. You may want them to include a pronunciation respelling with their sentences.

Library Skills

Objective To help students use a library database to locate books by title, author, or subject

Materials Any book that you have read from your school or local library, such as *The Bobbin Girl* by Emily Arnold McCully (4.2)

Lesson
1. Hold up the book you have chosen. Ask students, "What if you heard of this book and wanted to find it in your library? What could you do?"
2. Discuss students' responses. Possible responses include:
   - Ask the librarian.
   - Look on the shelves.
   - Use the card catalog.
   - Check the electronic database.

   Explain to students that they could hunt the shelves, but that the most efficient way to find a book in a library is to use the card catalog or the electronic database.
3. Describe the location and description of the card catalog or electronic database in your library. Tell students that there are three ways to look up a book in the catalog or on the computer: by using the book's *title*, the *author's name*, or the *subject* of the book. Using your book as a model, explain the following:
   - **Searching by Title:** If students are using a card catalog, tell them to look up the book alphabetically using the first word of the title. If the title begins with the word *the*, have students disregard this word and go to the second word. For example, to search for *The Bobbin Girl*, students would look under the letter *B*. Students using an electronic database can choose *Title* and then type in their response.
   - **Searching by Author:** Write the author's name on the board the way it would appear in the database, for example, *McCully, Emily Arnold*. Tell students to look under the author's last name when they search by author. If students are using an electronic database, they can choose *Author* and type in the author's name, using the author's last name first.
   - **Searching by Subject:** Remind students that *The Bobbin Girl* tells the story of a young millworker during a textile workers' strike in Lowell, Massachusetts. Explain that they would find *The Bobbin Girl* and other books about the same subject listed alphabetically under the subject headings *textile workers*, *strike*, or *Lowell, Massachusetts*. On an electronic database, students can choose *Subject* and type in the name of the subject.

4. Point out that since databases list books in three different ways, library users don't have to know everything about a book to find it in the library. Ask students how they might use their library database to solve problems such as the following:
   - What could I do if I loved this book by Emily Arnold McCully, and wanted to know if there were more books in the library written by her? (look up the author's name).
   - What could I do if I wanted to write a report about children working in mills and needed to read books about the topic? (look up the subject).
5. Show students the spine of the book you took out of the library. Point to the call number (or letters) on the spine. Tell students that the cards in the catalog or the list in the computer have the numbers or letters that match the numbers or letters on the book. Explain that this *call number* tells them where the book will be shelved in the library. With practice, they will be able to find the books they are looking for independently.

Status of the Class Follow-Up

As you take the Status of the Class, ask:
- What are the three ways that you could find your book in the card catalog or on the electronic database? (title, author, subject).
- If you were using the card catalog, what letter would you look under to find the title? The author?
- What subjects could you look up to find the title of your book?

Added Practice

- During your next library visit, send students on a scavenger hunt using the card catalog. Questions on your hunt might include:
  - How many books by Roald Dahl are in this library?
  - Name two titles of books about the Oregon Trail.
  - Who wrote the book *Well Wished*?
- Suggest that children begin a class database (card or electronic) to record classroom library books by title, author, or subjects. Help them determine how the database will be used so that they will be able to develop criteria for including books.

Note Taking

Objective To help students use the skill of note taking to understand and remember what they read

Materials Any nonfiction book related to a current theme of study, such as *Fossils* by Allan Roberts (4.5)

Lesson
1. Ask students, "Do you ever make a list or jot down notes outside of school? When and why do you do it?" Discuss students' responses and point out that many of their reasons for taking notes outside of school are also good reasons for taking notes as they read, for example:
   - To keep track of or organize information
   - To remember what they've read

2. Ask students, "What are some reasons that you might take notes in school?" Students' answers might include:
   - To prepare for a test
   - To gather information for a report

3. Hold up the nonfiction book (for example, *Fossils*) and say, "Suppose I am reading this book for a report that I'm writing on fossils. How would I go about taking notes on this book?"

4. Draw a blank concept web on the board and say, "Here are the steps I would follow to take notes on this book." As you describe the following steps, record examples in the web.

   Step 1. **Think:** Before I begin reading, I mentally review what I already know about the subject and what I want to learn. (Label the center circle with the subject, and some outside circles with questions, such as "What is a fossil?")

   Step 2. **Preview:** I look through the book, noticing headings and sub-headings. These tell me what ideas are being explained in the reading material. (Use headings to label additional circles in the web.)

   Step 3. **Read:** I read entire paragraphs or complete sections, making sure I understand them, before I begin taking notes.

   Step 4. **Write:** I pick out only the most important ideas to write down. Instead of copying exactly what's in the book, I write the ideas in my own words. (Record details in the appropriate circles.)

   Step 5. **Review:** I read over my notes to see if they are clear. If they are not, I add more information or rearrange how the information is organized.

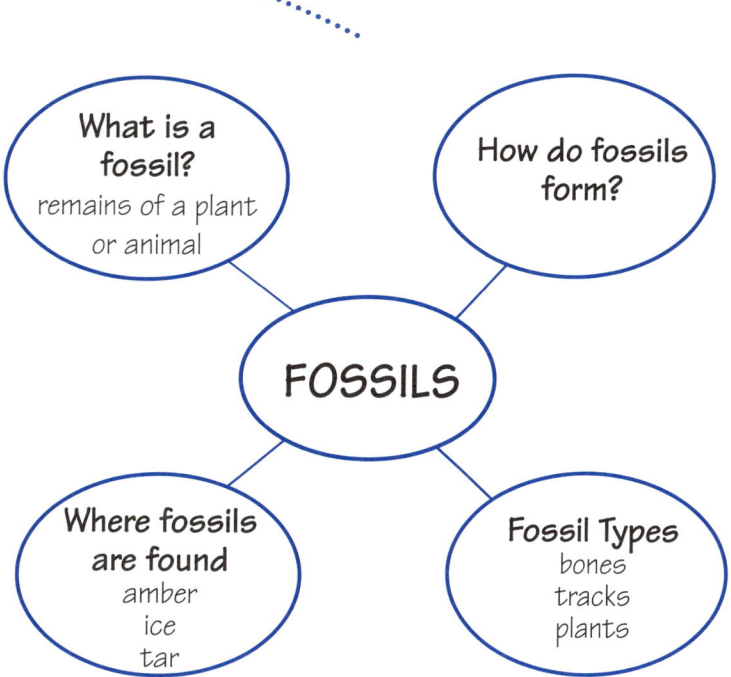

5. Tell students that they can pause and take notes any time they want to keep track of information or to help themselves remember what they have read. Remind students that they can add to or change their notes as they read.

Status of the Class Follow-Up

As you take the Status of the Class, ask:
- What reason might you have for taking notes on this book?
- If you were taking notes on this book, what information would you include?

Added Practice

- Students can use a diagram like the one shown to record notes on a book they are currently reading.
- Encourage students to take individual notes on note cards. After they have taken notes, have them organize the notes by dividing them into different piles. For example, students studying fossils may divide their notes into piles by categories such as fossil types, fossil formation, important fossil discoveries, and so on.

Parts of a Book

Objective To help students identify the table of contents and index and their uses

Materials Any nonfiction book with a table of contents and an index. The state books by Dennis Fradin, such as *Iowa* (4.3) have both. Optional materials: An overhead projector and transparencies of the table of contents and one page of the index

Lesson

1. Hold up the book you have chosen and ask students to imagine that they are looking for a book that covers particular topics. For example, if you are using one of the state books you might say, "Imagine that you are looking for a book about Iowa. You want to know about the geography and the history of the state. You also want to read about famous people who have lived in the state. How could you tell if this is the book for you?" Possible student responses might be:
   - You could begin reading.
   - You could skim through the book.
   - You could check the table of contents.

   Help students understand that the *table of contents* is a great tool to get a quick glance at what the book covers.

2. Open to the table of contents, showing students that it's in the front after the title page. (If you made transparencies, project a table of contents for students to see in more detail.) Point out that the table of contents lists chapters and the page on which each chapter begins. Read the chapter titles aloud. Ask, "Would this book likely have the information that you would need?" (yes).

3. Say, "What if I wanted to know if this book had very specific information about a certain topic? For example, what if I wanted to know if this book on Iowa has information on Fort Dodge? Where would I look then?" (the index).

4. Open the book or show the transparency of an index. Tell students that the *index* lists all of the topics in alphabetical order and can be a tremendous help in locating specific information. Point out that the numbers next to the topics show on what page or pages the information can be found. Ask, "Can I find the information I was looking for in this book?" (yes).

5. Direct students' eyes to a set of numbers, such as 24-26. Remind them that if a dash appears between two numbers, it means that the topic is discussed from the first page number to the last.

6. Tell students that using both the table of contents and the index can help them select books and find the information they are searching for.

Status of the Class Follow-Up

As you take the Status of the Class, ask:
- Does the book that you are reading have a table of contents or an index?
- If you were wondering if a sports book had a chapter on skateboarding, in what part of the book would you look? If you were wondering if a book mentioned a skateboard trick, where would you look?
- Have you ever used the table of contents or index of a book? What were you looking for? Was the table of contents or the index helpful?

Added Practice

- Challenge groups of students to a research scavenger hunt. Make a list of topics (both broad and specific) that you are currently studying. Have students find books that contain information on those topics. The first group to provide the names of books and the specific page where the information can be found wins the hunt.
- The next time your students write a report about a nonfiction topic, ask them to include a table of contents and an index. Developing an index helps students consider which key words might be useful for a reader, and helps them to understand which words may reasonably be found in an index.

Selecting Reference Materials

Objective To help students use reference materials to locate information

Materials Any book you are currently reading to students, such as *Mufaro's Beautiful Daughters* by John Steptoe (4.3); atlas, dictionary, several volumes of an encyclopedia

Lesson
1. Write on the board a number of factual questions that might be sparked by your current Read To book. For example, questions stemming from *Mufaro's Beautiful Daughters* might include:

   Where is Zimbabwe?
   Nyasha means "mercy." What does "mercy" mean?
   What would it be like to live in Zimbabwe now?

2. Ask students, "How might we find the answers to these questions?" Hold up the atlas, encyclopedia, and dictionary, and discuss the kind of information each one contains.
   - Atlas: maps and geographical information
   - Dictionary: spellings, pronunciations, and meanings of words
   - Encyclopedia: articles with general information about many subjects

3. Return to the questions on the board. Read aloud one of the questions and ask, "Would you be most likely to find the answer to this question in a dictionary, an encyclopedia, or an atlas?" Discuss students' reasons for their choices.

4. Ask students where they might find the answers to other questions on the list. Point out that it might be possible to find answers to some questions in two different references. For example, you could find information about where Zimbabwe is located in either an atlas or an encyclopedia. Discuss which resource would provide the most information.

5. Ask students to write down one or two questions that their reading has brought to mind. Tell students that you will be asking them how they might find the answers to their questions during Status of the Class.

Status of the Class Follow-Up

As you take the Status of the Class, ask:
- What questions did you write down about your book?
- Where might you find the answers to your questions?
- Could you find the information anywhere else? Which resource would give you the most complete information?

Added Practice

- Have students use index cards to write down factual questions that arise from their reading. Encourage them to use reference books to find the answers and record them on the cards.
- Suggest that small groups of students set up a "reference book scavenger hunt." Have each group write a list of ten questions that can be answered using an atlas, a dictionary, or an encyclopedia. Have the groups exchange lists and see how many of the questions they can answer. You may wish to arrange a study period in the school library for this activity, since students will need access to a variety of reference materials.

Using Maps and Charts

Objective To help students make inferences from maps and charts

Materials Any nonfiction book with a map or chart such as *Baseball in the Barrios* by Henry Horenstein (4.9)

Lesson
1. Read aloud a selection from the book that is supported by a map or chart.
2. Point out the map or chart to students. Tell students that writers and illustrators use maps and charts to give readers more information about a topic and to make information easier to understand. Point out that sometimes a map or chart helps to make the text clearer.
3. Open your book to a map or chart. Discuss the purpose of the map or chart and provide information on how to read it. For example, point out the map on the last spread of *Baseball in the Barrios*. Ask students, "Do you know what this star in the upper-left corner is?" (the compass rose). "What is the purpose of the compass rose?" (to show where north, south, east, and west are on the map). If there is a *map key* or *legend*, demonstrate how the key identifies each symbol on the map.
4. If you are focusing on a chart, help students read the titles and/or labels and determine how the chart is read. For example, using *Baseball in the Barrios*, you might show students the scoreboard in the front of the book. Explain that a scoreboard is a chart used in real life to illustrate how each team in a baseball game has performed. Ask students questions to guide them in making inferences using the map or chart. Try to ask questions that use or support the text. For example:
   - The author says that baseball is an *all*-American sport. He stresses the word *all*. Looking at the map, can you tell me what he meant? (Baseball is played in North and South America.)
   - What do you think the climate would be like in Venezuela? (hot and sunny, since it is near the equator). How would the climate in Venezuela affect the game of baseball? (It can be played all year round.)
5. Tell students that studying charts and maps before or while reading will help them to learn more about the subject at hand and often will make the text easier to understand.

Status of the Class Follow-Up

As you take the Status of the Class, ask:
- Are you reading nonfiction or have you read any lately that has a map or a chart?
- If so, what did you learn from the graphic? Did it help you to better understand what you were reading? Why or why not?
- Would a map or chart help you to understand what you are reading now? If so, what would you like to see?

Added Practice

- Have students search the local newspapers for maps or charts and post them on a bulletin board. Provide students with a list of questions that can be answered by studying the graphics.
- Invite students to draw a map of one of their favorite places. It can be a place that they frequent now or one that they visited when they were younger. Ask students to include a compass rose and map key. When maps are completed, pair students up to interview one another about their favorite places.

Reproducible Forms

Power Lesson Planning Form 92
Syllabication Rules 93
Student Reading Log 94
Primary Student Reading Log 95
Goal-Setting Chart 96
Sample TOPS Report 97
Student Reading Plan 98

Power Lesson Planning Form

Power Lesson Title

Objective

Materials

Lesson

Status of the Class Follow-Up

Added Practice

Syllabication Rules

RULE	EXAMPLES	YOUR WORDS
When two consonants come between two vowels, divide the word between the two consonants.	sum-mer win-dow	
When one consonant comes between two vowels, first try dividing the word before the consonant and giving the vowel a long sound. If that doesn't work, divide the word after the consonant and give the vowel a short sound.	do-nut mag-ic	
When a word ends with a consonant and *le*, divide the word before the consonant.	sim-ple ta-ble	

Reproducible Form © 2000, Renaissance Learning, Inc.

Student Reading Log

Student Name: _____ ZPD Range: _____

Title	Book Rdg. Level	Pts.	F/NF	Date	Pages Read in Class Begin-End	Pages Read out of Class Begin-End	% Correct	Teacher's Initials and Notes

Primary Student Reading Log

Student Name: _____ ZPD: Read To _____ Read With _____ Read Ind. _____

Date	Quiz No.	Title	Author	Book Rdg. Level	Initial One			Monitor's Initials	% Correct	Teacher's Notes
					Read To	Read With	Read Ind.			

Home Use — School Use

Reproducible Form © 2000, Renaissance Learning, Inc.

Goal-Setting Chart

Grade-Equivalent Score	ZPD		Point Values Expected from 60 Minutes per Day of Reading Practice			
	Average	Range	WK	6 WKS	9 WKS	YR
1.0	1.5	1.0-2.0	1.7	10	15	60
1.5	2.0	1.5-2.5	1.9	11	17	68
2.0	2.5	2.0-3.0	2.1	13	19	75
2.5	2.8	2.3-3.3	2.3	14	21	84
3.0	3.1	2.6-3.6	2.5	15	23	90
3.5	3.4	2.8-4.0	2.7	16	24	97
4.0	3.7	3.1-4.3	2.8	17	25	100
4.5	4.1	3.4-4.7	3.2	19	29	116
5.0	4.4	3.7-5.1	3.5	21	32	125
5.5	4.8	4.0-5.5	3.9	23	35	140
6.0	5.1	4.3-5.9	4.2	25	39	150
6.5	5.5	4.6-6.3	4.6	28	41	164
7.0	5.8	4.9-6.7	4.9	29	44	175
7.5	6.1	5.1-7.1	5.3	32	48	192
8.0	6.3	5.2-7.5	5.6	34	50	200
9.0	6.6	5.3-8.3	6.3	38	57	225
10.0	6.9	5.4-9.1	6.9	41	62	250
11.0	7.2	5.5-9.9	7.6	46	68	275
12.0	7.5	5.6-10.7	8.3	50	75	300

This chart is a guideline only. Both grade-equivalent scores and book readability levels are approximations. Use your professional judgment to adjust ZPD ranges to match individual students, taking into account such factors as a student's prior knowledge, appetite for challenge, interest, and need for variety. When moving students to higher levels, consider suggesting shorter books.

Reproducible Form © 2000, Renaissance Learning, Inc.

TOPS Report for Jeremy Wallace
Accelerated Reader®: Friday, March 26, 1999

Lincoln Elementary

Class: Language Arts 5   **Teacher:** Strout, B.
ID: 83-1165   **Grade:** 5   **Team:** Lions

Magnificent, Jeremy! You have passed quiz number 5449 on the book <u>Will You Sign Here, John Hancock?</u> by Jean Fritz.

Quiz Results

Book Level: 4.1
Number Correct/Possible: 9 / 10 (90.0%)
Points Earned/Possible: 0.9 / 1.0
Read Independently
Fiction

Marking Period Results to Date (100% of MP- 3)

		Marking Period Goal	
Average Book Level:	4.0	4.1	
Average Percent Correct:	78.2%	85%	
Points Earned:	24.2	29.0	(83.4% of goal)
Quizzes Passed/Taken:	11 / 11	--	

School Year Results to Date (75% of school year)

Average Book Level: 3.6
Average Percent Correct: 77.8%
Points Earned: 67.5
Quizzes Passed/Taken: 34 / 36

Certification Level

Last Certification & Date	Current Certification Goal
Advanced Reader (2) 3/24/99	Advanced Reader (3)

Monitor Signature   Teacher Signature

Comments:

STUDENT READING PLAN

Student_____ Grade_____ Teacher_____
Grade-Equivalent Score/Test Date_____ _____ _____
School Year_____ Beginning ZPD: Average_____ Range_____

1 BOOK-LEVEL GOAL

Marking Period	Goal	Actual
1	_____	_____
2	_____	_____
3	_____	_____
4	_____	_____
5	_____	_____
6	_____	_____

2 POINT GOAL

Marking Period	Goal	Actual
1	_____	_____
2	_____	_____
3	_____	_____
4	_____	_____
5	_____	_____
6	_____	_____

3 MINIMUM AVG. % CORRECT

Marking Period	Goal	Actual
1	_____	_____
2	_____	_____
3	_____	_____
4	_____	_____
5	_____	_____
6	_____	_____

4 CERTIFICATION GOAL*

Marking Period	Ind	Sup	Adv	Sta	Cla	Hon
1						
2						
3						
4						
5						
6						

Fill in the bottom half of the box to indicate a goal.
Fill in the whole box when you reach the goal.

5 OTHER GOALS

Marking Period	Goal	Actual
1	_____	_____
2	_____	_____
3	_____	_____
4	_____	_____
5	_____	_____
6	_____	_____

COMMITMENT TO GOALS

Marking Period	Student Signature/Date	Teacher Signature/Date	Parent Signature/Date
1	_____	_____	_____
2	_____	_____	_____
3	_____	_____	_____
4	_____	_____	_____
5	_____	_____	_____
6	_____	_____	_____

* **Certification Codes:** Ind=Independent Reader, Sup=Super Reader, Adv=Advanced Reader, Sta=Star Reader, Cla=Classic Reader, Hon=Honors Reader.

Reproducible Form © 2000, Renaissance Learning, Inc.

List of Books Referred to in the Lessons

Fiction
101 Ways to Bug Your Parents by Lee Wardlaw, 78-79
Aunt Nancy and Old Man Trouble by Phyllis Root, 22-23
Belle Prater's Boy by Ruth White, 76-77
The Bobbin Girl by Emily Arnold McCully, 80-81
Charlotte's Web by E.B. White, 46-47, 50
Coyote and the Laughing Butterflies by Harriet Taylor, 22-23
Earth to Matthew by Paula Danzinger, 18-19
Ella Enchanted by Gail Carson Levine, 24-25
The Family Under the Bridge by Natalie Savage Carlson, 64-65
The Fighting Ground by Avi, 55
The Fortune-Tellers by Lloyd Alexander, 34-35
Frindle by Andrew Clements, 21
Good Times on Grandfather Mountain by Jacqueline Briggs Martin, 32-33
Harry Potter Books by J.K. Rowling, 21
Holes by Louis Sachar, 52-53
Mufaro's Beautiful Daughters by John Steptoe, 86-87
My Brother Sam Is Dead by James Lincoln Collier and Christopher Collier, 54-55
Number the Stars by Lois Lowry, 62-63
Pegasus, the Flying Horse by Jane Yolen, 56-57
Poppy by Avi, 70-71
Sarah Bishop by Scott O'Dell, 55
Snowdrops for Cousin Ruth by Susan Katz, 66-67
Stone Fox by John Reynolds Gardiner, 50-51
The True Story of the Three Little Pigs by Jon Scieszka, 23
Walk Two Moons by Sharon Creech, 21
Well Wished by Franny Billingsley, 81
The Wheel on the School by Meindert DeJong, 68-69
The Wizard of Oz by L. Frank Baum, 50
A Year With Butch and Spike by Gail Gauthier, 62-63

Nonfiction
26 Fairmount Avenue by Tomie DePaola, 60-61
Baseball in the Barrios by Henry Horenstein, 88-89
Call Me Ahnighito by Pam Conrad, 12-14
The Earth by Cynthia Pratt Nicolson, 18-19
Earthwise at School by Linda Lowery and Marybeth Lorbiecki, 18-19
Ellis Island by Patricia Ryon Quiri, 26-27
Fossils by Allan Roberts, 82-83
The Honey Makers by Gail Gibbons, 20-21
If You Traveled on the Underground Railroad by Ellen Levine, 30-31
Iowa by Dennis Fradin, 84-85
An Island Scrapbook by Virginia Wright-Frierson, 36-37
The Magic School Bus Inside the Earth by Joanna Cole, 18-19
Outside and Inside Birds by Sandra Markle, 38-39
Pocket Pets by Alvin and Virginia Silverstein, 44-45
A River Ran Wild by Lynn Cherry, 40-41
Rosa Parks by Eloise Greenfield, 60-61
Weird Animals by Tammy Everts, 42-43
What Happened to the Dinosaurs? by Franklyn M. Branley, 28-29
Why Don't You Get a Horse, Sam Adams? by Jean Fritz, 55
Will You Sign Here, John Hancock? by Jean Fritz, 10-11

Poetry
"Birches" by Robert Frost, 48-49
"Crocodile" (Anonymous), 58-59
"The Crocodile" by Michael Flanders, 58-59

Index of Skills Taught

*Concepts and skills that are the subject
of specific power lessons are shown in bold type.*

Antonyms, 64-65, **68-69**
Atlas, 86-87
Author's purpose, 18-19
Author's style, 46-49, 58-59
Autobiography, 60-61
Biography, 60-61
Book selection
    selecting reference materials, 86-87
    using the card catalog, 80-81
    using ZPD, 7-9
Card catalog, 80-81
Cause and effect, 32-33
Characterization, 24-25, **50-51**
Charts, 88-89
Classifying and categorizing, 20-21, 82-83
Clue words, 64-65, 68-69
    for generalizations, 30-31
    for sequence, 40-41
Compare and contrast, 22-23, 63
Conclusions, drawing, 24-25
Conflict and resolution, 52-53
Consonant variants, 70-71
Context clues, 64-65, 68-69, 78-79
Description, 46-47
Details
    in summaries, 42-43
    main idea and, 28-29, 42
    that support characterization, 24-25
    that support conclusions, 24-25
    that support predictions, 34-35
    that support setting, 54-55
Dialogue, 24-25
Dictionary, **78-79**, 86-87
    pronunciation key and respellings using,
    78-79, 86-87
Electronic database. *See* Card catalog.
Encyclopedia, 63, 86-87
Fact and opinion, 26-27
Fiction, 18-19, 62-63
Figurative language
    imagery, 46-47

    similes, 48-49
    metaphors, 48-49
Fix-up strategies. *See* Self-correction
    strategies.
Following directions, 40-41
Folktales, 22-23
Generalizations, making, 30-31
Genre, 15, 23, 60-63
    autobiography, 60-61
    biography, 60-61
    folktales, 22-23
    historical fiction, 62-63
    poetry, 48-49, 58-59
    realistic fiction, 62-63
Goal setting, 15-17
Goal-Setting Chart, 15-17; reproducible, 96
Graphic organizers
    causes and effects chart, 32
    compare and contrast chart, 22
    concept web, 83
    homonym chart, 66
    K-W-L chart, 37
    main idea and details chart, 29, 42
    plot diagram, 52
    prediction chart, 34, 65
    prefix diagram, 72
    suffix chart, 74
    theme diagram, 57
    Venn diagram, 19, 63
    word web, 21, 68
Graphic elements
    in previewing text, 37
    maps and charts, 88-89
Headings and subheadings, 20-21, **44-45**,
    82-83
Historical fiction, 62-63
Homographs, 64-67, 79
Homonyms, 66-67
Imagery, **46-47**, 48-49, 58-59
Indexes, 84-85
Inferences, making, 24-25

about author's purpose, 18-19
about causes and effects, 32-33
about characters, 24-25, 50-51
about fact and opinion, 26-27
about generalizations, 30-31
about setting, 54-55
about tone, 58-59
from author's style, 46-49, 58-59
from context clues, 64-65
from maps and charts, 88-89
to predict outcomes, 34-35
Library skills, 80-81
card catalog, 80-81
electronic database, 80-81
selecting books, 7-9, 80-81
selecting reference materials, 86-87
Main idea, **28-29**, **42-43**
and details, 28-29, 42-43
in summaries, 42-43
Maps, **88-89**, 55, 86-87
Metaphors, **48-49**
Multiple meanings, words with, 66-67
Nonfiction, 20-21, 26-27, 42-43, 60-61, 84-85
Note taking, 44-45, **82-83**
Order of events, 40-41
Parts of a book, 36-37, **84-85**
Persuasive writing, 18-19
Phonics
consonant variants, **70-71**
syllabication, **76-77**
VCCV words, 76
VCV words, 76
Plot, **52-53**
and setting, 54-55
and theme, 56-57
conflict and resolution, **52-53**
Poetry, 48-49, 58-59
Predicting outcomes, **34-35**, 50
Prefixes, **72-73**
Pre-reading skills, 36-37
Previewing, **36-37**, 44, 82
Prior knowledge, using
as self-correction strategy, 38-39
in drawing conclusions, 24-25

to predict outcomes, 34-35
Pronunciation key, 86
Reading Renaissance, **7-17**
setting goals, **15-17**
using the student reading log, **12-14**
using the Student Reading Plan, **15-17**
using the TOPS Report, **10-11**
using zone of proximal development (ZPD), **7-9**
Realistic fiction, 62-63
Reference materials, **45**, **86-87**
selecting, **86-87**
text features in, 44-45, 88-89
Root words, 72-75
Self-correction strategies, **38-39**
context clues, 38-39
fix-up strategies, **38-39**
Sequence, **40-41**
Setting, 46-47, **54-55**, 62-63
Setting a purpose, **36-37**
Similes, **48-49**
Student reading log, 8, **12-14**, 15;
reproducibles, 94-95
Student Reading Plan, 15-17;
reproducible, 98
Suffixes, **74-75**
Summarizing, **42-43**
Syllabication, **76-77**
prefixes, 72-73
rules, **76-77**; reproducible, 93
self-correction, 38-39
suffixes, 74-75
Synonyms, 64-65, **68-69**
Table of contents, **84-85**
Text features
headings and subheadings, 44-45
illustrations, 36-37
maps and charts, 88-89
Theme, 23, **56-57**, 62-63
Tone, **58-59**
Topic, 18-19, 23, 28-29, 80-81, 84-85
TOPS Report, **10-11**; sample, 97
Vocabulary strategies, 64-69
Context clues, **64-65**

101

    Homonyms, 66-67
    Synonyms and antonyms, 68-69
Word study, 72-77
    prefixes, 72-73
    suffixes, 74-75
    syllabication, 76-77
Writing
    descriptions, 46-47
    directions, 40-41
    literature dialogue journal, 25
    paragraphs, 26-27, 58-59, 64-65
    poetry, 48-49
    reports, 84-85
    story endings, 52-53
    summaries, 42-43
Zone of proximal development (ZPD), 7-9, 12-14, 15-17

Index of Accelerated Reader Literacy Skills Taught

Initial Understanding

Describing actions or events. *See* Sequence, 40-41, and Plot: conflict and resolution, 52-53.

Identifying reasons. *See* Characterization, 50-51.

Recognizing details. *See* Main idea and details, 28-29.

Recognizing feelings. *See* Tone, 58-59, and Drawing conclusions, 24-25.

Understanding dialogue. *See* Drawing conclusions, 24-25.

Understanding sequence. *See* Sequence, 40-41.

Literary Analysis

Recognizing plot. *See* Plot: conflict and resolution, 52-53.

Recognizing setting. *See* Setting, 54-55.

Understanding the author's craft. *See* Imagery, 46-47; Similes and metaphors, 48-49; and Tone, 58-59.

Understanding characterization. *See* Characterization, 50-51, and Drawing conclusions, 24-25.

Understanding historical/cultural factors. *See* Historical fiction, 62-63, and Setting, 54-55.

Understanding literary features. *See* Theme, 56-57, and Tone, 58-59.

Inferential Comprehension

Comparing and contrasting. *See* Compare and contrast, 22-23.

Drawing conclusions. *See* Drawing conclusions, 24-25.

Extending meaning. *See* Making generalizations, 30-31; Imagery, 46-47; and Similes and metaphors, 48-49.

Making inferences. *See* Drawing conclusions, 24-25; Author's purpose, 18-19; Predicting outcomes, 34-35; and Multiple causes and effects, 32-33.

Making predictions. *See* Predicting outcomes, 34-35.

Recognizing cause and effect. *See* Multiple causes and effects, 32-33.

Constructing Meaning

Deriving word or phrase meaning. *See* Context clues, 64-65, and Synonyms and antonyms, 68-69.

Differentiating fact and opinion. *See* Fact and opinion, 26-27.

Identifying persuasive language. *See* Author's purpose, 18-19.

Identifying reading strategies. *See* Self-correction strategies, 38-39, and Context clues, 64-65.

Responding to literature. *See* Author's purpose, 18-19; Imagery, 46-47; and Tone, 58-59.

Understanding the main idea. *See* Main idea and details, 28-29.

Renaissance™ Resources for Teachers

More than 300,000 educators nationwide have come to trust Renaissance seminars and materials for their professional development. Shown below are some of our most popular resources.

Seminars

Our highly acclaimed seminars in reading, early literacy, math, test strategies, and classroom management produce immediate results for both you and your students. Seminars take place in hotels or can be brought to your facility. Call for details today! (800) 338-4204, ref. #4905S.

Teaching Resources

The Basics of Reading Renaissance® Video Kit

While there's no replacement for a live seminar, this video kit is a wonderful introduction for new teachers joining a Reading Renaissance staff, and a great refresher for those already trained. You'll learn proven techniques for helping every student become a successful reader.

For AR™ 5 and above; call for earlier versions.
ISBN 1-893751-75-9
Includes four videos (106 min. total) and *Trainer's Guide*.
Item #TS88-3115K $595.00

Diagnosis & Intervention Video Kit

Learn how to pinpoint and solve student reading problems quickly, before students become frustrated. This kit introduces classroom-proven techniques to provide individualized support for every student, regardless of reading level.

For AR 5 and above; call for earlier versions.
ISBN 1-893751-77-5
Includes two videos (54 min. total) and *Viewer's Guide*.
Item #TS88-3130K $199.95

Duolog Reading™ Book

Improve fluency and build confidence with this breakthrough peer-tutoring technique! It's so easy to learn, you can quickly train elementary, middle, and high school students—as well as parents and volunteers—as tutors. Great for emergent readers who are developing basic skills, hesitant readers who require extra support, and skilled readers ready for extra challenge.

ISBN 0-9646404-5-7
Item #TS88-3068 $16.95
SAVE! Buy 10 or more for only $14.95 each!

44 Routines Book

This small book of routines will make a big difference in your classroom right away! You'll learn effective new ways to take attendance, give assignments, collect homework, and deal with behavior problems, creating a smooth-running classroom where students learn more.

ISBN 1-893751-61-9
Item #TS88-3088 $8.95
SAVE! Buy 10 or more for only $7.95 each!

To request a catalog or place an order, call us today!

(800) 338-4204, ref. #4905S